CW00952009

STUNNING

S T I T C H E S

WITH ORIGINAL PATTERNS

STUNNING
S T I T C H E S
WITH ORIGINAL PATTERNS

PRIMROSE SULLY

Illustrated by Sandy Ross

MEREHURST

LONDON

Published 1990 by Merehurst Limited
Ferry House, 51/57 Lacy Road,
Putney,
London, SW15 1PR

by arrangement with Primrose Sully
First published in Australia by
William Heinemann Australia

ISBN 1-85391-172-0

Illustrations by Sandy Ross
Designed by Nuttshell Graphics

Typeset in Australia by
   Midland Typesetters, Maryborough
Produced by Mandarin Offset
   in Hong Kong

Contents

To my mother, who patiently taught and encouraged me from early childhood to appreciate and above all to enjoy the wonderful pastime of embroidery. She was a talented needlewoman who gave pleasure to so many people with her creations.

To Chrissie, who spent many hours also patiently teaching and encouraging me.

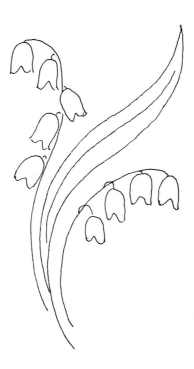

Lily of the Valley Pillow Slip (page 48), *Two Continental Pillows* (page 87, page 95)

Bullion Roses and Posy on Towels and Washer
(page 19)

Sachet (page 14), *Shoe Bag* (page 26), *Collars*
(page 55) *and Coat Hangers* (page 71)

Baby's Nightgown (page 32), Baby's Dress (page 111) and Crib Blanket (page 40)

Camisole (page 92), *Knickers and Half Slip* (page 60)

Bridge Cloth (page 100), Decorative Beaded Ornaments (page 128) and Door Stop (page 76)

Bed Jacket (page 66)

Nightgown (page 120)

Beaded Sweater (page 135) Inset Sloppy Joe with Ribbon Roses (page 106)

Author's Note

My most heart-felt thanks must go to Michael Meredith who unwisely volunteered to type this manuscript for me in his spare time. He has valiantly ploughed through reams of mostly illegible scribblings, deciphered them correctly, corrected spelling and patiently retyped many alterations. His advice was often sought and generously given. My thanks also go to his wife, Jill, a very fine embroiderer, who has not only sustained Michael, with numerous cups of coffee, but also offered loads of encouragement to me.

I would also like to thank Sandy, my talented daughter-in-law, for her beautiful diagrams and illustrations into which she put so much thought and effort to capture the flavour and feeling of the embroidered items. I also got to know and love a warm and delightful person.

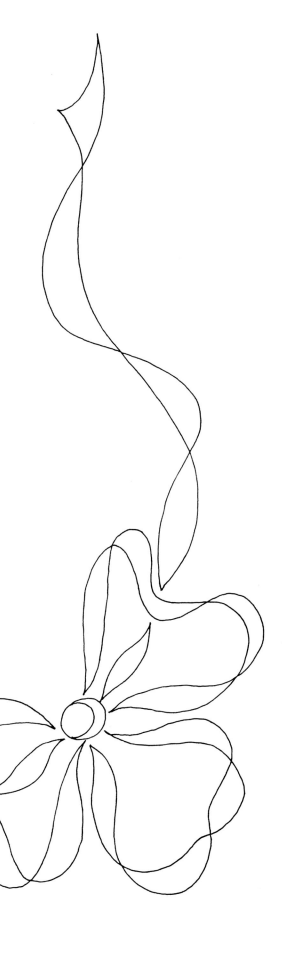

Introduction

One never feels lonely with embroidery for company. I can think of few things I would rather do than settle down in front of the fire in winter, or in a shady spot in the summer with a new project to work on. It is the most soothing, yet at the same time stimulating and exciting, feeling to be creating your own design and there is quite a sense of achievement when it's finished.

For the last few years I have been teaching and sharing with others the pleasures I have enjoyed and it is so rewarding to see the satisfaction others derive from this creative pastime. I would not presume to set myself up as an expert on embroidery as there are many books that provide expert guidance, but my students have said constantly that they simply don't understand the books or know where to begin. The stitches look wonderful but, as beginners, they don't know how to use them. In my classes I start with a simple handkerchief sachet and work through a beginners course and then take students through an advanced course. My aim with this book is also to start off with simpler projects and work through to more complicated ones, while trying to remove some of the mystery.

My students want to know what needle, how many threads, how many stitches? Unfortunately I am not at all exact by nature, so I find these questions quite difficult, as to me the questions should be answered a little by trial and error. After all, one will achieve quite a different effect by, for instance, increasing the number of threads used. However, with each item covered in this book I specify all the details, including size of needle and number of threads, but please, dear reader, experiment yourself as well—that is half the fun.

How to Use this Book

To gain the maximum enjoyment from this book, please, before you embark on any of the projects, READ the text thoroughly right through from beginning to end of that particular chapter. You will then find the instructions easier to follow once you begin to work and be able to relate the text to the diagrams as you go.

The first five projects in this book form the basis of my beginners course. They deal with quite a number of the basic fine embroidery stitches and their application to practical use. Please begin with the first project if you are a novice and work your way gradually through the book. You will find by the time you reach the sixth project, the lily of the valley pillow, that although there are some new techniques, the later pieces are all refinements of the early ones and by this time you will be quite experienced. One point I cannot stress enough: PRACTICE MAKES PERFECT. If you think you have not mastered a particular stitch, keep working at it, and you will find that it suddenly becomes easy.

Another very important point is your eyesight. You may or may not wear glasses for normal everyday use, but I have found that fine work is nonetheless quite taxing on your eyes and you may need to strengthen your glasses or sit in a very good light to work. I have found a marvellous lamp without which I would be lost. It is made by Luxo Australia (in England by One Thousand and One Lamps and in America by Luxo). It is called the Argus and has either a weighted base or a clamp base to screw onto the table. A long extendable arm makes positioning over your work easy and you look at it through a magnifying glass lit from underneath by a light globe.

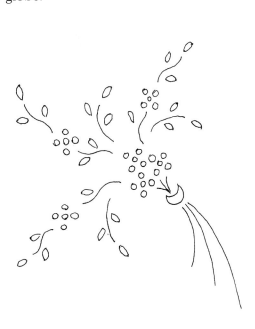

For some projects I have recommended particular colour numbers for embroidery threads, but they are intended as a guide only. My students have asked me to include them, as they assure me it helps to be guided at first.

The last ten items in the book are individual projects and are not listed in order of complexity, the exceptions being the baby's dress and adult nightgown. I believe a beginner would find these techniques difficult without first completing the earlier projects in the book. One needs to acquire a degree of confidence before embarking on these two projects, particularly mastering the rolling and whipping technique.

All the measurements in the book are given in metric, with imperial equivalents in brackets. It is very important that, for each project, you follow one set of measurements only and not mix them together. The adult clothing sizes are given in bust or waist measurements as appropriate, in both metric and imperial, to avoid the confusion that might arise in different countries from using a dress size.

On all the diagrams, shading indicates the WRONG side of material. A seam allowance is included on all patterns.

I wish you all every success and hope I am able to impart through this book my knowledge of and my enthusiasm for this wonderful and rewarding pastime.

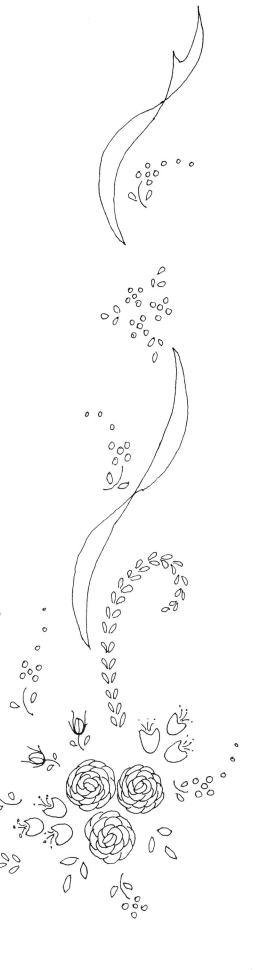

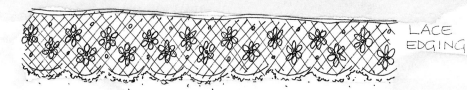

BRODERIE
INSERTION

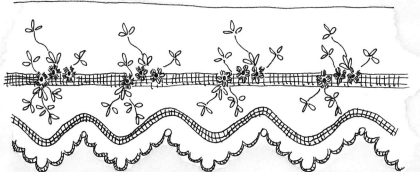

LACE
EDGING

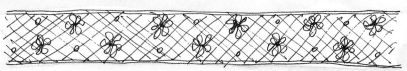

BRODERIE
EDGING

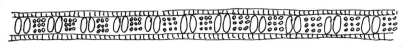

LACE
INSERTION

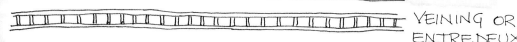

BRODERIE
BEADING

VEINING OR
ENTREDEUX

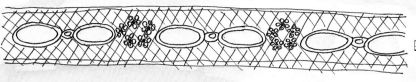

LACE
BEADING

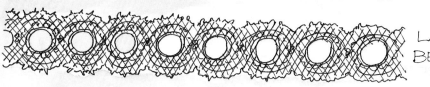

LACE
BEADING

Kit and Kaboodle

The basic requirements for embroidery are very few and they may be purchased here and there as you need them. I have had some of my tools for so long I can't really remember when I acquired them, and if you are interested in sewing and embroidery, the chances are you already have most of the bits and pieces necessary.

Materials

Laces, ribbons, cottons, fabrics and so on are the main requirements. Always choose good quality fabric, ribbons and laces. Embroidery is time-consuming and it is a shame to put so much time and effort into creating something beautiful only to find after a few washes that it looks like a rag. Pure fabrics are the best: cotton voiles, linen, silk organza, bastiste, cotton velveteen and pure wool. They are so much better to work with too. The only exception I make is with ribbons and laces. Good quality French laces usually have 10 per cent nylon in them, which is a great advantage as the lace does not require ironing but at the same time does not frizzle when the iron catches it. Good laces have become very expensive and as a result are hard to find. If you do find a good selection it is worth stocking up. These little pieces never go astray. I have included a sketch of the types of laces referred to in the book so you will know how to identify them. Polyester satin ribbon seems to be the best available today. There are several varieties, some more rigid and stiff than others. I prefer the softer one, it washes beautifully and requires no ironing. The beautiful old pure silk double-sided satin ribbons seem to have gone forever; if you are lucky enough to find some in Granny's work basket or an antique shop, treasure them, as they were far superior to anything we can purchase now.

One more point I would like to make is that the finished appearance of your embroidered garment depends not only on the quality of embroidery but also on the finishing touches. Large, ugly french seams and bias bindings can completely ruin what would otherwise be a beautiful garment. Keep the seams fine and trim the bias bindings back so they are narrow. If you compare the two you will see what I mean. And press studs, unless completely hidden, are a NO NO. Replace them with buttons and buttonholes if possible—it is worth the extra effort in the long run.

Stranded Cottons
I use DMC stranded cottons as I like the colour range and quality. For some of the projects in this book I refer to individual colour numbers, but please don't feel restricted. This is only supposed to be a guide.

To pull a thread from a new skein of cotton, draw the thread from the middle of the skein. It usually hangs out from the skein and is the obvious one to pull. Pull it in the direction of the hands shown on the lower band. Make a mistake, however, and you will regret the resulting tangle!

The easiest way to remove the correct number of strands for embroidery is to select the length you require and cut the whole thread right through. Remember which end you cut, as this end will be threaded through the eye of the needle. Separate out the number of threads you require by holding the two amounts of thread in the right hand, say two threads in one bundle and four threads in the other. Leave the tail of cotton free for untwisting and run the index finger of your left hand slowly down between the two bundles of thread to separate them. Thread the needle with the end you have cut from the skein and the thread will keep its natural twist and sheen. It will also knot and tangle less.

Wools
DMC have a lovely range of tapestry wools, which are used for the fifth project, the crib blanket. Appletons also have an exciting range of colours in their crewel wools. These are used on the beaded sweater. Individual colour numbers are given as a guide only. You can use one or more strands of this wool to achieve varying effects.

Tools

Magnifying Glasses and Lights
I find I need a little extra help, especially at night, to see what I am embroidering clearly. If you are using tone on tone it can be particularly difficult, but fortunately there is help at hand in the form of two marvellous aids. One is a magnifying glass that can be hung around your neck, suspended by a cord, and propped against the chest. The other is the portable magnifying light made by Luxo and mentioned in How to Use this Book. These are extremely useful for very fine work.

Handpainted
pine
needlecase

Needles

I seem to have a vast collection of needles in varying sizes and thicknesses stuck into a pin cushion or the arm of my favourite chair. I really only need three or four packets and could throw the rest away. I use Milward needles in my classes. There are some variations in the needle sizes of different brands, but all the numbers used in the book are Milward. The higher the needle number, the finer the needle.

For fine hand sewing I prefer a no. 10 crewel needle, but in this book I have recommended you use a no. 9 crewel. This is really a compromise, as the no. 9 is much easier to thread than the no. 10 and in my classes we all agreed to settle for the no. 9.

Straw needles are available in an assortment of sizes from 3 to 9 in the one packet. The no. 3 may be used for six strands of embroidery thread and the no. 9 for one strand. Straw needles are particularly helpful for working bullion stitch (on the washer, project 3, for instance), as the shaft of the needle is long enough to accommodate the twists of thread and the eye is tapered into the shaft of the needle so it doesn't snag or catch when pulling through. Straw needles are also used for beading.

Chenille needles also come in an assorted pack, from size 18 to 24. The size 18 may be used for tapestry wool and the 24 for crewel wool. These needles have a large eye for threading and a sharp point for piercing the fabric.

The other very long needle, about 9 cm (3½ in) long, I have mentioned in two of the chapters I found in an assorted pack of needles in a supermarket.

Stiletto or Tailors Awl

These are available from your haberdasher or some of the large department stores. A stiletto or tailors awl is a pointed metal tool of graduated thickness, usually with a wooden, bone, plastic or silver handle. You may be fortunate enough to possess an antique one. This tool is used to pierce the fabric and make a hole. The size of the hole will depend on how far into the fabric you push the shaft of the stiletto. It is possible to make an eyelet hole in fine fabric just by wiggling a needle round in a circle in the space between the threads, but I find using a stiletto is easier.

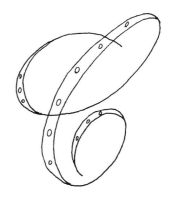

Tape Measure

The best tape measure to have is a flexible one with inches one side and centimetres the other, which makes it easy to do a quick conversion if you are like me and still think in inches but have to purchase and work in metric. In this book, all measurements are given in both metric and imperial systems. Follow one set of measurements only; DO NOT mix them in one project.

Finger Shield

I have never used one of these, but I am told they are very helpful worn on the index finger of the left hand to prevent digging up the skin on that finger whilst working.

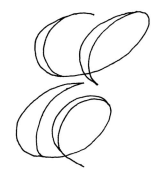

Scissors

It is very important to have a fine-pointed pair of small, sharp embroidery scissors on hand. These need to be kept hidden at all times from marauding children and husbands, who will want to borrow them for snipping fingernails, wire etc. A large pair for cutting out are also necessary.

Loop Turner

This is the most brilliant tool and its inventor deserves a medal. It makes turning a fine rouleau a breeze. It is truly an essential part of your kit and kaboodle. Loop turners are available from most haberdashery shops.

Thimble

I am lucky enough to have my mother's silver thimble, and I truly can't sew without it. But this is rather an individual thing and whether you use a thimble seems to depend on when and how you were taught. It seems to be a practice I acquired in childhood, so perhaps it is more difficult to get used to if you are a late starter. It saves puncturing the end of your second finger, especially when working heavier cloth. If you can't manage one, don't worry; many fine embroiderers amongst my students don't use a thimble.

Transferring Designs

Transferring a design is sometimes quite a difficult procedure, especially when the fabric is opaque. A number of methods are, however, available.

Water-Soluble Felt-Tipped Fabric Marking Pens

If the fabric is sheer and the design can be traced, these pens are ideal. It is very important, however, that the chemical in the ink is washed right out of the fabric so the marks don't keep reappearing. I have found the best way is to hold the fabric under a running cold-water tap to rinse away every vestige of chemical.

Fade-Out Marker Pen

This pen, combined with tailors chalk or dressmakers carbon, is very useful when working with velveteen. The fade-out pen marks disappear within forty-eight hours or may be washed out in cold water. To transfer a large design onto velveteen, trace off the design onto transparent tracing paper then use dressmakers carbon to transfer it to the fabric then reinforce the design by going over it with a fade-out pen. The carbon lines by themselves tend to disappear while the work is being carried out. The advantage of the fade-out pen is that the finished article doesn't need washing to remove the design lines.

Tailors Chalk

Tailors chalk is useful for marking out a design on woollen fabrics. Again dressmakers carbon may be used first and the design reinforced with chalk. If the chalk has not rubbed out completely by the time you have finished working the design then try a stiff brush or soak in cold water.

Dressmakers Carbon Paper

This is very useful for transferring designs onto an opaque fabric. The carbon is placed between the design and fabric (carbon side to fabric), and the design is traced with a tracing wheel, pencil or pointed stick. The carbon can later be washed out.

Using Light

A satisfactory method for transferring designs to rather opaque fabrics is to outline the design on paper with a darker line, for example with a black felt-tipped pen, and tape it to a window in daylight hours. Then tape the fabric over the top of the design. The design lines should be quite visible and can be traced onto the fabric with a water-soluble fabric marking pen. A light box can also be used. A light is placed under a glass sheet with the design and fabric on top of the glass.

Tracing Pencils

A variety of dressmakers pencils are available, some of chalk, some oil-based, some transfer by heat. I seldom use them, as I prefer the other methods described above. I also sometimes use an ordinary pencil to trace a design, very lightly marking the pattern.

Additional Designs

An alphabet has been included for you to trace off monograms for the continental pillow and coat hanger or any other projects where you would like to include an initial.

Some additional designs have also been included for you to try alternative decoration for some of the projects.

This design could be worked
in shadow stitch in single
thread

1 Sachet

Materials

23 cm (9 in) x 107 cm (42 in) silk organza
1.8 m (2 yds) x 25 mm (1 in) lace edging
¼–½ cup lavender
Water-soluble fabric marking pen
Stranded cottons: two shades of your chosen colour for bow and daisies, and green
No. 9 crewel needle

New Stitches and Techniques

Stem stitch
Satin stitch
Lazy daisy stitch
Gathering, whipping and applying lace (Method 1)
Overcasting stitch

A lavender-scented sachet or stocking bag is always a useful gift. I begin this book with very simple stitches and apply them in this manner to demonstrate that even the simplest of stitches can look very professional. Don't feel limited either. If you enjoy making the sachet, you may like to apply some of the stitches in later projects instead of the ones used here. For example the bow could be worked in shadow stitch, tiny bullion roses substituted for daisies, and the leaves satin stitched.

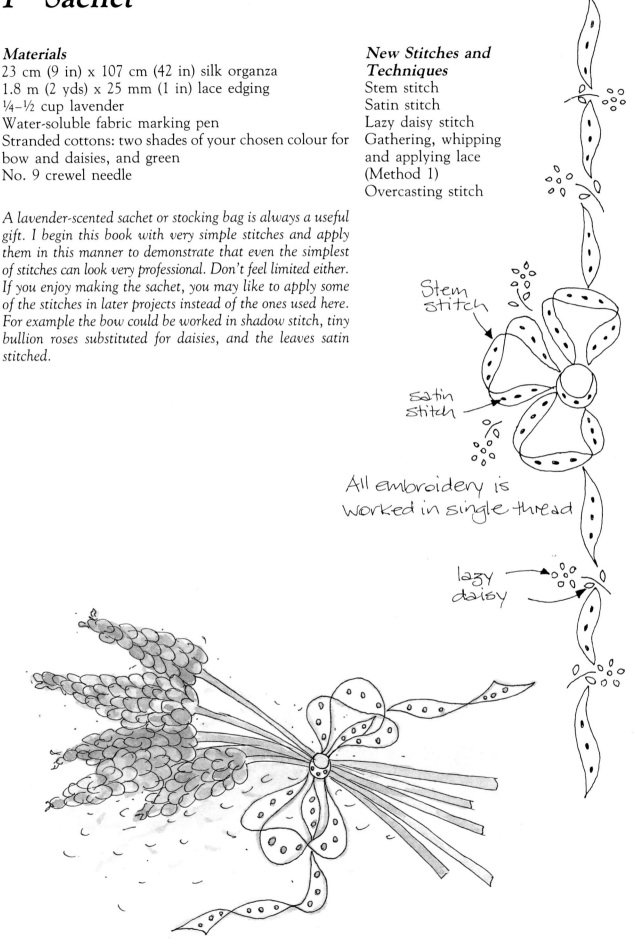

Stem stitch

Satin stitch

All embroidery is worked in single thread

lazy daisy

To begin, fold a strip of organza in half, selvedge to selvedge, and sew the raw edges together at the sides by machine. Trim the seam back to 3 mm (1/8 in), turn and press. The selvedge edges are left open. Centre the drawing of the bow 4.5 cm (1¾ in) above the selvedge and, with the loops of the bow facing away from the selvedges, trace the design onto the material with a water-soluble felt marking pen. Thread a no. 9 crewel needle with a single strand of the colour you have chosen for the bow (no knot). Cut the thread no more than about 60 cm (24 in) as it tends to knot and fray. You are now ready to commence sewing. Sew through both thicknesses of fabric to form a sewn line that will prevent the lavender falling through when the sachet is finished.

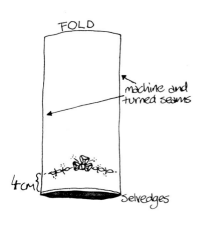

Hold the work in your left hand over the index finger, and with the second finger acting as a stabilizer, run three LITTLE running stitches towards you along the right hand side of the ribbon segment. Then commence stem stitch, working back over the running stitches. This will secure the thread so you will not need to knot it.

Stem Sitch

The thread stays to the right hand side of the needle all the time. Place the needle in at A and bring it out at B. The needle emerges at B just above the top of the previous stitch. This makes a neat, fine line. (If a thicker line is desired in another project, bring the point of the needle out just below and to the left of B.)

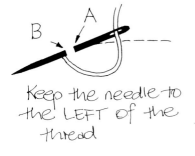

Keep the needle to the LEFT of the thread

When you reach the end of the first little segment of ribbon, end with a very small stitch, then turn your work so it faces completely the other way and stem stitch back to the beginning. Take the thread to the back of the work, without ending off, bring the needle back up to the front one-third of the way along, and work little spots in the middle of the ribbon by making four little satin stitches into the same two holes.

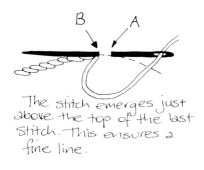

The stitch emerges just above the top of the last stitch. This ensures a fine line.

Satin Stitch

The needle goes in at A and comes out at B. Keep the thread to the right of needle. The thread may be carried between the spots, but not between segments of ribbon. To end off, do three little stitches into the back of one of the spots, place your thumb on top, give a gentle tug and cut the thread. Finish ribbon bow in this manner too.

The little daisies are worked into the breaks in the ribbon to prevent lavender falling through into the main body of the sachet. Select a colour for the flowers, use a single thread again, and commence with the centre of the daisy, working four or five satin stitches then working the petals in lazy daisy stitch. Hold your work so that the petal you are about to work is between you and the centre of the daisy.

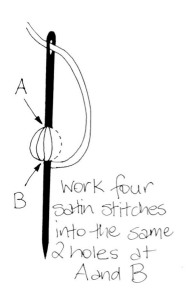

Work four satin stitches into the same 2 holes at A and B

Lazy Daisy Stitch

The needle goes in at A and comes out at B. The thread is held in place with the thumb while making the stitch, so that the thread remains under the point of needle. Pull the needle through and anchor the stitch by putting the needle back down over the thread at B and emerging again at C ready to work the next petal.

The stems are worked in single thread stem stitch and the leaves in lazy daisy.

Once you have worked the whole design, rinse the sachet to remove the blue pen, dry and press.

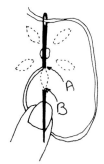

Trim the selvedge edge by cutting through half its width and straighten the edge if this is necessary. Turn the raw edges 5 mm (¼ in) to the inside and press. Tack the edges together, leaving an opening at one end. Fill the space loosely with lavender and close the opening with tacking.

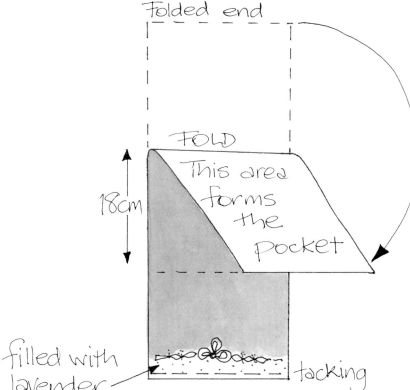

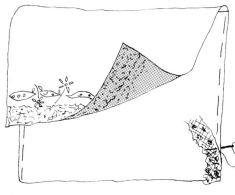

Attach lace to organza RIGHT sides together

Gathering, Whipping and Applying Lace

Fold up the fabric wrong sides together from the folded end to make a pocket about 18 cm (7 in) deep and tack the sides together, making sure that both edges are even.

Take the piece of lace and, with the straight side to your left, make a small double hem on the wrong side, commencing work from the scalloped edge and finishing at the straight edge. Don't end off. Place the straight side of the lace against the tacked edges of the organza, right sides together, with the small hem at the bottom of the sachet. Secure the lace to the sachet by overcasting for approximately three stitches through all thicknesses. Then place the needle into the LACE ONLY, about 3 mm (1/8 in) further on and draw the needle through, pulling the cotton so the lace forms a small pleat. Secure this pleat with one stitch through all thicknesses and continue in this manner, working two or three overcasting stitches through all thicknesses between pleats until the desired fullness is achieved. Extra gathering should be allowed when rounding corners. This process not only whips the lace to the sachet but also securely closes the sachet's sides.

When the end of the pocket is reached, the lace must be folded towards the OUTSIDE of the sachet and whipping continued—form the pleat this time by just pushing it into place with your finger. The process of turning the lace to the inside of the sachet is repeated again when the other side of the pocket is reached. End off the lace at the bottom with another small double hem.

To press the lace, hold a steam iron just above the lace, barely touching it and gently persuade the lace to lie away from the edge of sachet, without pressing the lace flat.

overcasting

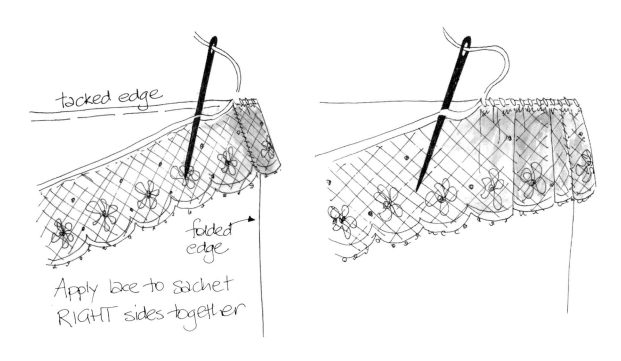

tacked edge

folded edge

Apply lace to sachet RIGHT sides together

2 Bullion Roses and Posy on Washer

Materials

1 towelling face washer
35 cm (14 in) beading
60 cm (¾ yd) polyester satin ribbon to fit the beading
Packet size 3/9 straw needles; no. 9 crewel needle
Stranded cottons:
   3 shades pink (DMC 223, 224, 225) or selected
   colour for your rose
   Green (DMC 3051) for leaves
   Blue (DMC 800) and yellow (DMC 727) for forget-
   me-nots

New Stitches and Techniques

Bullion stitch (grub rose)
Forget-me-nots
Fly stitch
Ribbon bow

The grub, or bullion, roses are a very popular embroidery design. The variations are endless for the actual bullion stitch, but I would like to deal with, in particular, the round, full-blown roses, so popular on washers and towels.

There is a secret to achieving a healthy, silky full-blown appearance, which will be explained in greater detail further on. The main points to keep in mind while you are working are:

1. keep the twisting loose,
2. put more twists on the needle than appear to be necessary, and
3. twist the embroidery cotton clockwise around the needle (to keep the sheen on the cotton).

I am not in favour of counting twists, as the number of twists will differ depending on the SIZE OF THE STITCH taken into the fabric. The twisting must be sufficient to cover this distance. The twists need to be an even tension, quite loose, and firmly packed—for example, a 1 cm stitch would require approximately twenty loose twists. The larger the stitch, the more twists required. Once the needle is pulled through the twists and the thread pulled tight, the twists compact and the bullion stitch becomes rounded and raised up.

Holding your work correctly is all important too. Two methods work well.

HAND TOWEL

Design is spread over 18cm

LARGE BATH TOWEL

Design is spread over 33cm

20

Method 1

Hold the work in your left hand, so that the area to be embroidered is directly over your index finger. Use the second and third fingers to grip the rest of the work securely in the palm of your hand, leaving your thumb free to help stabilize the needle and pack down the twists. The work must be held firmly, to create tension on the fabric while twisting the thread.

Method 2

First anchor the thread with a small backstitch, then take first stitch into the fabric, pushing the needle well through. Hold the needle between the thumb and forefinger of your left hand and commence twisting the thread round the needle. When pulling the needle through the twisting, release the tension from the washer and place your thumb firmly over the twists to keep them all in order while you are pulling the needle through.

The straw needles are especially well suited to this purpose as they have a long tapered shaft, the eye does not protrude at the sides so there is less risk of the needle snagging when you are pulling it through the twists, and there is plenty of shaft on which to twist the thread. If you find these needles difficult to purchase, ask your local haberdashery shop to order them in for you. If you get the packet of 3/9 needles, you can use the no. 3 needle for six strands, right down to one strand in the no. 9 needle. Let's now begin.

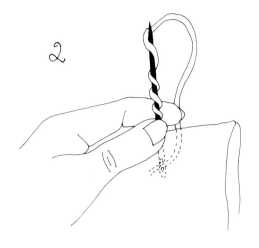

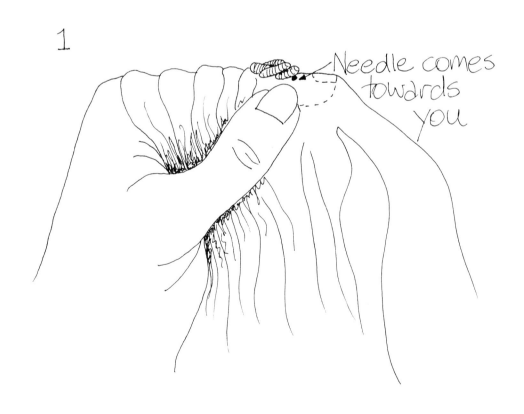

Needle comes towards you

Bullion Stitch

Fold the washer into four and, with the label to the back, commence work in the middle of one quarter. This will be the centre of the rose. Thread the largest straw needle in the packet with the full six strands of the deepest shade of embroidery cotton, threading the needle from the cut end to keep the natural twist in the thread. Make a back stitch in the washer to secure the thread, then put the needle in at A taking it through the washer to emerge at B. Be sure to push the needle well through. THE DISTANCE BETWEEN A AND B WILL BE THE SIZE OF THE FIRST BULLION.

Holding the thread closest to the point of the needle, commence twisting clockwise around the needle, keeping an even, quite loose tension, making sure the first twist is well down at the base of the needle, otherwise the thread tends to look messy when the stitch is finished.

Once the thread is pulled through the middle of the bullion, the loosely twisted threads will compact, but tightly twisted ones have no room to compact and will instead buckle.

Once you have completed the twisting, place your thumb over the twists, holding them firmly in place and gently pull the needle through. Still keeping your thumb over the threads, ease your centre thread towards A, thus pulling the finished bullion stitch into place. Keep the tension quite firm by giving the needle a little extra tug. This will compact all the threads and the bullion stitch will lie firmly on the washer.

Finally, secure the stitch by going back down at A and coming up again just next to B at C, to commence the next bullion stitch for the centre of the rose.

Once the second bullion is completed to lie right beside the first one, end off the thread by taking the needle to the back of your work and making three small stitches into the threads; place your thumb on top, give a little tug and cut the thread.

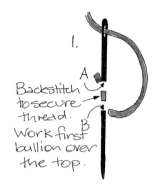

1.

Backstitch to secure thread.
Work first bullion over the top.

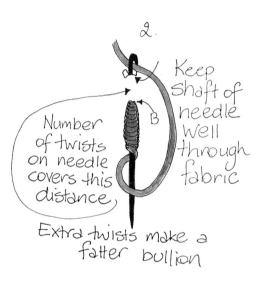

2.

Number of twists on needle covers this distance

Keep shaft of needle well through fabric

Extra twists make a fatter bullion

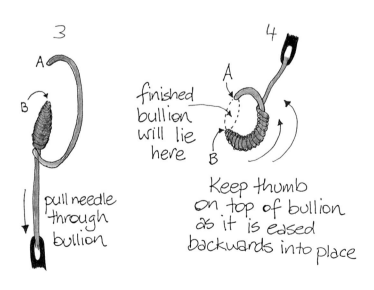

3

pull needle through bullion

4

finished bullion will lie here

Keep thumb on top of bullion as it is eased backwards into place

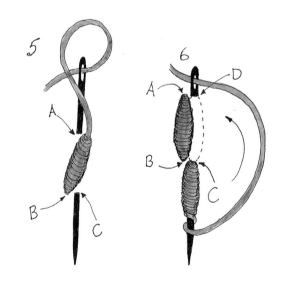

5

6

Thread the next deepest shade of cotton, still using six strands and the same needle. Secure the thread into the stitches on the back of the work, bringing the point of the needle through to the front, half way along the first bullion stitch, at E. Pull the needle and thread right through.

Put the point of the needle down at F and bring it back out at E and commence twisting. Make this stitch a little longer, with a few extra twists, as it has to lie in a slight semi-circle.

When securing bullions from now on, put the point of the needle down at the end of a completed bullion. Then bring the needle out half way along the newly completed bullion and pull the thread through. This must be done before commencing the next bullion. This anchoring stitch is essential and, if it is forgotten, there will be an unattractive thread lying on top of your work next to the bullion.

The rest of the rose is worked in this manner, working anti-clockwise around the rose, placing the last bullion in the circle to overlap the point at which you started the circle.

Work one more round in the palest shade of embroidery cotton. Secure the thread into the back of the work and bring the needle up on the outside, half way along one of the previous bullions. Work each bullion between this point and the half way point of the next bullion in the previous round. If the bullions have been successfully completed and appear rounded and plump, these two rounds should be sufficient.

Once you have completed your rose, you can look forward to finishing off the rest of the posy. Work two buds by placing two bullion stitches next to each other so that the base of each bud points towards the rose. These are worked in six strands in the second deepest shade.

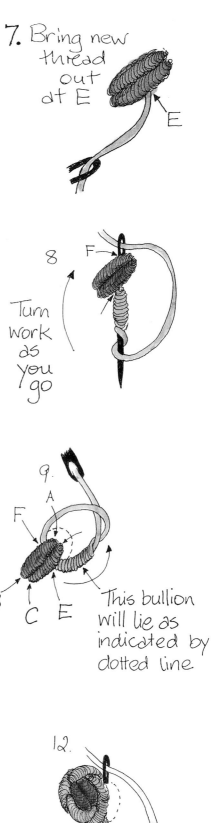

7. Bring new thread out at E

E

8

Turn work as you go

F

9.

F

A

B C E

This bullion will lie as indicated by dotted line

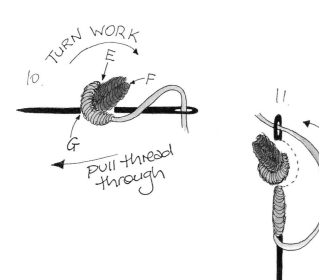

TURN WORK

10.

E

F

G

Pull thread through

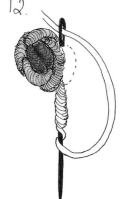

11.

12.

Forget-me-nots

These flowers are worked in three strands of the blue stranded cotton using a no. 9 crewel or a straw needle. The forget-me-nots are worked in quite close to the rose. Commencing at A and bringing the needle up at B, work four satin stitches into the same two holes. The distance between A and B is about 5 mm (¼ in).

Bring the needle out at B, turn your work, place the needle in at C, and work four more satin stitches into C and B. Continue in this manner until you form a small square. The centre of the square is worked in three strands of yellow thread and not more than four satin stitches. End the work with three backstitches into the back of the work.

Now for the stems and leaves. These are worked in three strands of the green stranded cotton again using a size no. 9 crewel or a straw needle. Commencing at the bottom of the stem, work the first stem in stem stitch, working a nice curve and finishing just below the middle of the rose. Slip the thread through the back of the rose to emerge at the top of the main rose and continue stem stitch to the base of one of the buds. Push the needle down at A and up at B, and pull the needle through. Hold the thread down with your thumb at A, and take it around the bud. Push the needle in at C and bring it back out at A so that the thread is around and under the needle (fly stitch). To anchor the stitch place the needle point in at D. Repeat the fly stitch a little below and a little wider and shorter than the first one.

While you are in the vicinity of the bud you can work a couple of leaves by making three or four satin stitches into the same two holes and encasing them in a lazy daisy stitch. The leaves are then worked in this way in little groups of twos and threes, with the base of the first two leaves forming a V and the third in the middle. Complete the rest of the stems and leaves.

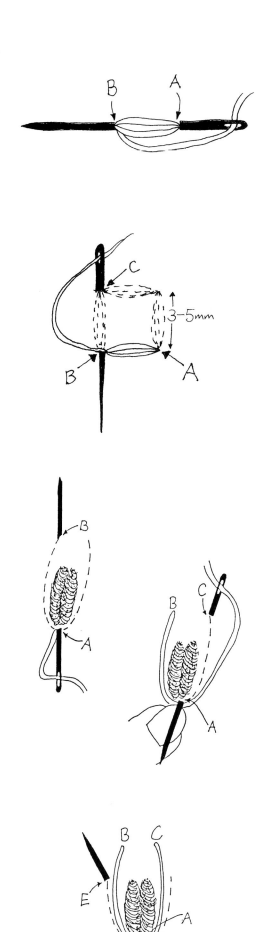

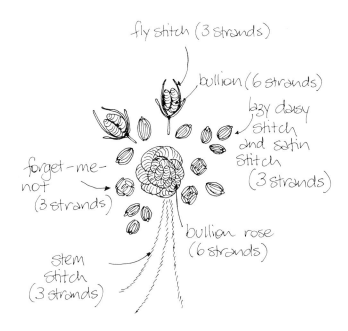

fly stitch (3 strands)

bullion (6 strands)

lazy daisy stitch and satin stitch (3 strands)

forget-me-not (3 strands)

bullion rose (6 strands)

stem stitch (3 strands)

24

Ribbon Bow

The finishing touch is a length of beading lace backstitched with matching thread to the washer and threaded with ribbon wide enough to thread through the beading and of an appropriate colour caught at both ends so it is secure for washing. The bow is made separately using approximately 25 cm (10 in) of ribbon.

Form a figure 8 keeping the satin side of the ribbon to the front all the time. Holding the ribbon between the thumb and forefinger of your left hand, form a loop with your right hand. Transfer the loop to your right hand and use your left hand to form another loop, taking the tail behind the first loop. Transfer the bow to your left hand and, with a needle and knotted thread, pass the needle through the centre section of the bow, catching all the loops and winding the cotton around the centre a couple of times; pull the thread tight and place the needle back down through the ribbons to the back. Stitch the bow into place on the beading beneath the rose.

Hand towels and bath towels can be worked in a similar fashion, and suggested designs are included for these.

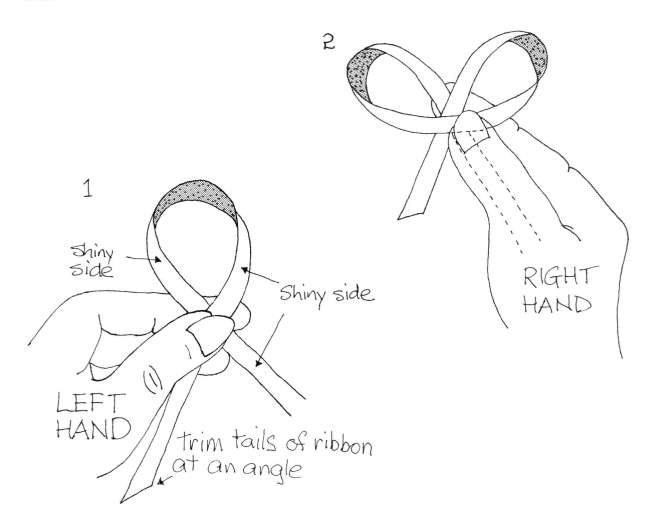

1

Shiny side

Shiny side

LEFT HAND

trim tails of ribbon at an angle

2

RIGHT HAND

3 Shoe Bag

Materials
35 cm (14 in) x 107 cm (42 in) silk organza
1.8 m (2 yds) x 3 mm (1/8 in) polyester satin ribbon
Stranded cottons: one colour for bow, one for flowers, and one for leaves
No. 9 crewel needle
Water-soluble fabric marking pen

New Stitches and Techniques
Blanket stitch
Satin stitch flowers (two threads)
Dots
Eyelets
Shadow work
French seams

I have chosen to work shadow stitch on organza for this lesson as the organza is so sheer that the stitches are clearly visible and become a feature. It is almost better if the stitches are not too small in this particular case, as the stitches themselves create quite an impact if they are kept neat and even. For finer work and a less sheer fabric, a more shadowy effect is created by making the stitches closer together.

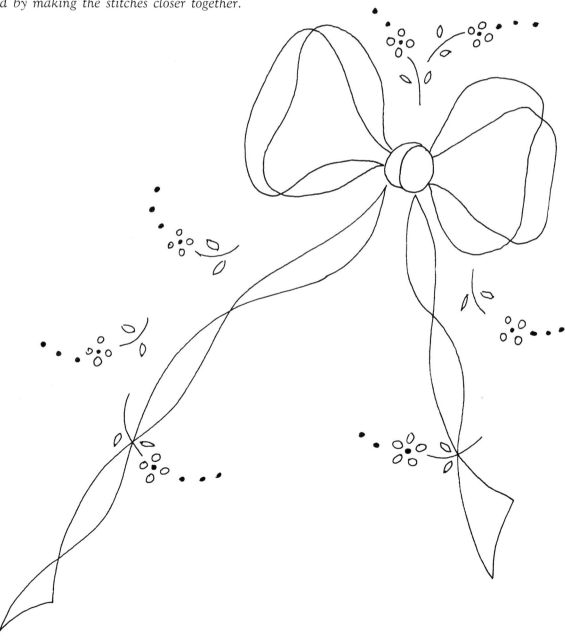

Fold the organza in half, placing the selvedges together, and press the fold with your thumb. Make a second fold lengthwise and make another crease. Open out the fabric and centre the material over the bow design using the long crease as a guide. Place the longest tail of the bow about 3 cm (1¼ in) from the bottom crease with the loops of the bow towards the selvedge. Trace the design onto your material using a water-soluble pen.

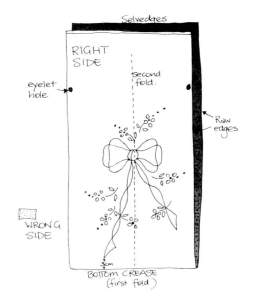

Shadow Work

Thread a no. 9 crewel needle with two long strands of stranded cotton. I prefer to work shadow stitches from the back and this is the method I describe, although it can also be worked from the front. (Shadow stitch is herringbone stitch worked on the wrong side of the fabric.) Commence by holding the work so the wrong side faces you and the design to be worked points away from you. Work three little running stitches along the right hand side of the line towards you (these will be worked back over with the shadow stitch). Work shadow stitch by placing the point of the needle in at A and up out at B. Keeping the thread to the right of the needle come across to the other side of the design and put the needle in at C and out again at B. Now put the needle in at D and out again at A. Go across to the other side and put needle in at E and up at C. If in doubt as to where the thread should be whilst taking a stitch, lie the thread down the middle of the area to be shadow stitched to the right of the work. Continue in this manner, always keeping the thread out to the right hand side before taking a stitch and always linking up the stitches so that on the right side of the work it will look like a line of small back stitches. Be very careful not to pull the thread tight while working, otherwise the material underneath the threads will buckle.

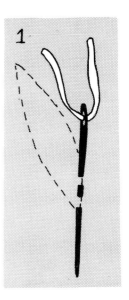

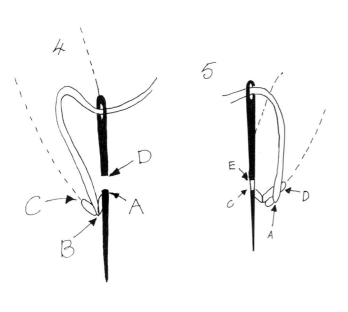

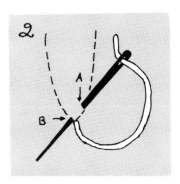

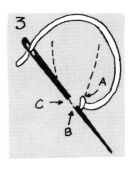

To finish off the shadow stitch, darn the thread back along the side edges of a few completed shadow stitches, through the embroidery threads only, on the wrong side. To begin another thread, darn the end back along the sides in the same manner as for the ending off and just continue on. Constantly check your work on the right side to make sure there are no gaps between stitches.

Where there is a curve in the design, the inner curve is worked in slightly smaller stitches and the outer curve in slightly larger stitches so continuity is maintained. Where there is a single line to be worked, for example, in the centre of the bow, the single line is worked in stem stitch on the back of the work, but be careful to link up each stitch; it will look the same as the shadow stitch on the front of the work. Similarly, if you run out of room to shadow stitch but still have an incomplete line, use stem stitch to complete the line.

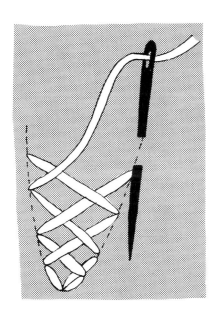

Use stem stitch on back of work to complete the line

Flowers

Using two strands of embroidery cotton and a no. 9 or 10 crewel needle, hold the work over your index finger, with the centre of the flower closest to you. Commence work on petal farthest from you. Place the needle in at A and out at B (B is at least 1 mm or 1/16 in from the centre) and pull the tail of the cotton almost to the end. This tail of cotton will darn into the work eventually. Place the needle back in at A, forming the first small stitch. Bring the needle out at C, down again at D, up at E, and down at F. This makes three little stitches side by side into different holes to form the base of the petal. Bring the point of the needle up again at B and continue working only between B and A, being careful not to let the point of the needle creep up or down, as this would create the wrong shape. Work over the petal about eight times in total, including the first three stitches, using your thumb to spread the stitches to left and to right before they come to rest. This should give you a nice round petal shape. You will notice that the petal has grown considerably, so you should take care to make the initial three stitches very small, keeping the base at least 1 mm (1/16 in) from the centre to allow room for a centre to be worked when the flower is finished. Work four or five petals in this manner. The centres and dots are worked in a similar fashion to petals, but a single thread only is used. Each dot or centre must be fastened off securely behind with three little stitches or a knot. The stitches of the dots should point along the line of dots to keep continuity.

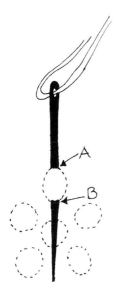

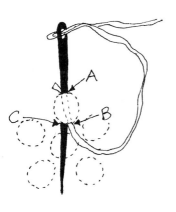

Stems and Leaves

These are worked in single thread with a no. 9 crewel needle starting at the base of the stem and working towards the flower in stem stitch. When the stem is completed, take the needle through to the back of the work and darn down the stem through stitches until you arrive in place to do a leaf. Bring the needle up at the base of the leaf and work three or four satin stitches, and work a lazy daisy stitch around the outside of each petal.

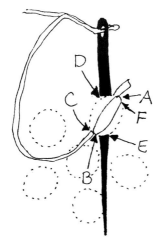

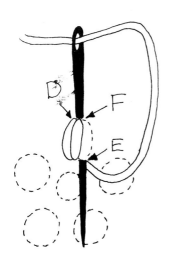

Eyelets

With the embroidery completed, the eyelets for the ribbons should be prepared next. Measure down 15 cm (6 in) from the edge of selvedge (I leave selvedges on in this case, as they are stronger and less likely to fray) and 1.5 cm (5/8 in) in from the edge punch a hole with a tailors awl or stiletto. You will need four holes altogether, two in the front and two in the back. The holes need to be large enough to accommodate the 3 mm (1/8 in) ribbons.

To work the eyelets, thread a no. 9 crewel needle with machine cotton and overcast the edge of the hole, gently working approximately three threads into the fabric and turning the work as you go. When the overcasting is finished blanket stitch over the overcasting to form a firm eyelet. To end off, darn the threads through the back of the stitches.

To Make Up

Place selvedges together and, with the right side out, machine stitch down both sides. Trim the edges to about 3 mm (1/8 in). Turn the bag inside out and machine down both sides again, enclosing raw edges (french seam). Leave the bag inside out and press a 7.5 cm (3 in) hem down at the top centring eyelets just above the hem edge. Machine around the edge of the selvedge below the eyelets and machine another row above the eyelets to form a casing for the ribbon. Turn right side out. Cut the ribbon in half and thread one piece of ribbon through the front right-hand eyelet around and out at the back right-hand eyelet. Knot the ends of the ribbon together. The other piece is threaded through the left hand side all around, emerging at the left-hand side again, and knot its ends. The ribbons form the draw string.

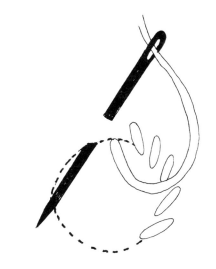

OVERCASTING STITCH

BLANKET STITCH

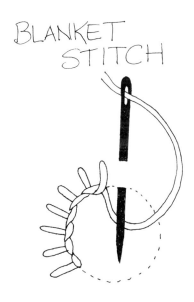

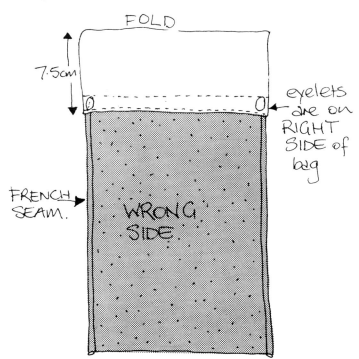

FOLD

7.5cm

eyelets are on RIGHT SIDE of bag

FRENCH SEAM.

WRONG SIDE

FRENCH SEAM

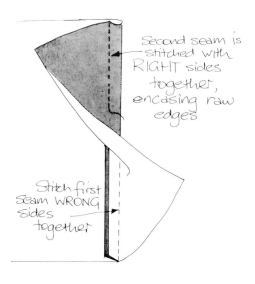

Second seam is stitched with RIGHT sides together, encasing raw edges

Stitch first seam WRONG sides together

31

4 Baby's Nightgown

Materials

90 cm (1 yd) x 115 cm (45 in) cotton voile
1.2 m (1¼ yds) narrow lace for neck and sleeves
1 m (1¼ yds) x 6 mm (¼ in) ribbon
53 cm (21 in) x 20 mm (¾ in) insertion lace
5 buttons, 10 mm (3/8 in) diameter
Stranded cottons (any colours)
No. 9 crewel needle

New Stitches and Techniques

Satin stitch leaf
(Method 1)
Drawn thread hem-
stitching
Rolling and whipping
and attaching lace
Joining lace
Feather stitch
Blind hemming
Buttonholes

I have included this baby's nightgown to demonstrate a variety of simple stitches and their application to clothing. The same techniques can be applied to a number of commercial patterns, such as a blouse or nightdress. The baby nightgown could also be reversed, with an adjustment for the neck, leaving the front free for embroidery. The hem is cut straight, so threads could be drawn at the hemline and the hem secured with drawn thread work. There are so many possibilities, but here are some ideas to make a start.

Sleeves

Fold the sleeves in half lengthwise and machine the seams (french or overlocked seams), matching the notches. Sew the sleeves into the nightgown.

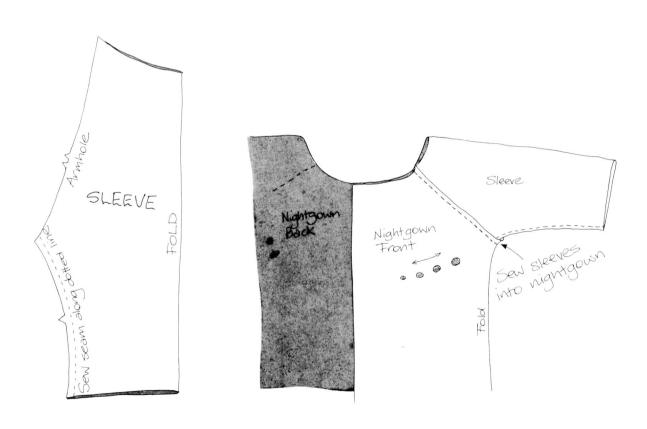

Front Bands

Make a 5 mm (¼ in) fold to the wrong side of the two front bands and press. Fold again to the wrong side on the fold line and press. Along the hemstitch line indicated on the pattern, gently draw six threads out of the fabric, one at a time, from the neck to the hem, using a fine needle or pin.

To mark the buttonholes on the right front band, measure 2 cm (¾ in) down from the neck edge and place a dot in the middle of the band. This represents the middle of the first buttonhole. Mark four more buttonholes with 7 cm (2¾ in) between each one, taking the measurement from the centre of one buttonhole to the centre of the next one. Draw a line through the middle of each dot to represent the buttonhole so as not to confuse the markings with embroidery design markings.

Measure half way between each buttonhole (3.5 cm, or 1 3/8 in) and mark with a dot. Open out the front band and trace the design, using a water-soluble pen, centred on the dot between the buttonhole. The embroidery is worked first, through one thickness of the material, before the bands are hemstitched into place.

The satin stitch flowers are worked in the same way as on the shoe bag, but this time use a no. 9 or 10 crewel needle with a single thread of stranded cotton and work each petal with about twelve stitches. Work three little flowers interlocking with each other.

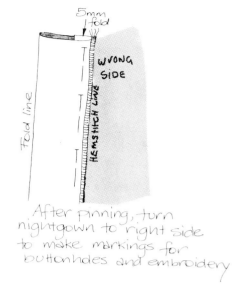

After pinning, turn nightgown to right side to make markings for buttonholes and embroidery

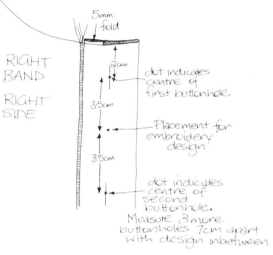

RIGHT BAND
RIGHT SIDE

5mm fold

2cm — dot indicates centre of first buttonhole.

3.5cm

Placement for embroidery design

3.5cm

dot indicates centre of second buttonhole.

Measure 3 more buttonholes 7cm apart with design inbetween

Design for front band

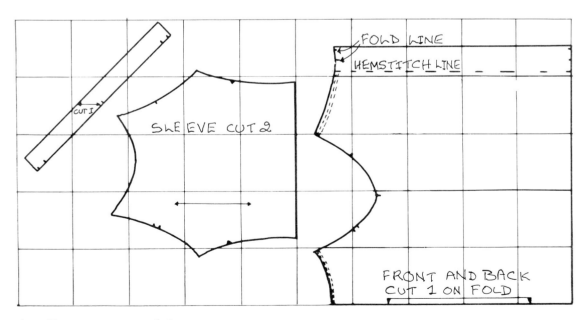

FOLD LINE
HEMSTITCH LINE
SLEEVE CUT 2
CUT 1
FRONT AND BACK
CUT 1 ON FOLD

1 Square = 10 cm
1 cm Seam Allowance
One size only

Satin Stitch Leaves Method No. 1

The leaves are then worked into the three spaces between the flowers. Use a no. 9 crewel needle and a single thread of stranded cotton. Commence the leaf by working three running stitches A to B. Work five satin stitches (for padding) over the running stitches. Work a lazy daisy stitch around the satin stitches and bring the needle up again at B. Now work satin stitch across the padding, commencing at B, at the point of the leaf, with three tiny satin stitches through the padding stitches only. Fill the rest of the leaf with satin stitches, this time through the fabric. Finish with three tiny satin stitches into the padding stitches only at point A. Take the needle through to the back and end off each leaf.

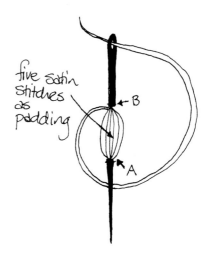

Drawn Thread Hemstitch

Once the embroidery is completed, tack the folded band in place right to the edges of the drawn threads. Using machine cotton and holding the band with the hem closest to you, commence from the right hand end with a few small stitches into the hem to secure thread. Collect a small bundle of threads on the needle from A to B – collect no more than a square of drawn threads or puckering will occur.

Draw the needle right through, then insert needle back into the first hole again at A, take it back to B and this time bring the needle out, just catching the hem at C, level with where previous stitch emerged. The work will pucker if you make this stitch any further along the hem. The sewing thread must not be caught around the needle during the second step.

Complete the left front band in the same way, omitting the embroidery and buttonholes.

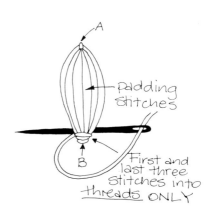

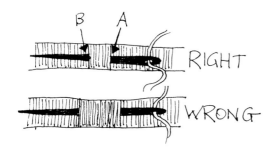

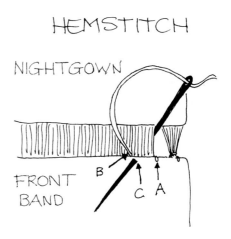

Rolling, Whipping and Attaching Lace

To finish the edge of each sleeve, trim the raw edges so they are neat and not frayed. Thread a no. 9 crewel needle with machine cotton and knot the end of thread. Place the needle parallel with the edge of the sleeve over the seam and, with the dampened finger and thumb of your left hand, apply considerable pressure and roll the fabric over the needle, bringing the needle up in the middle of the roll so that the knot is hidden within the roll. Now place the right side of the lace to the right side of the sleeve, leaving a tail of 5 mm (¼ in), and with the inside of the sleeve facing you, commence to roll the fabric and whip the lace onto the edge of the sleeve by taking the needle over and coming up under the roll each time, completely encasing the roll in the thread and catching the lace in at the same time. The needle is inserted into the lace about the width of the needle from the straight edge. Keep the tension on the thread very firm, as this is essential for a neat finish.

To join the ends of the lace, fold the bottom raw edge towards you with the WRONG sides of the lace together. Now fold the top raw edge with the RIGHT sides of lace together. Place the top fold over the bottom raw edge to form an overlapping seam and tuck in the raw edges. Hem along both folds, once on the RIGHT side and once on the WRONG side.

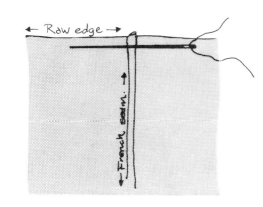

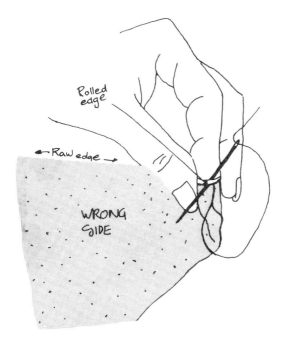

ROLLING AND WHIPPING

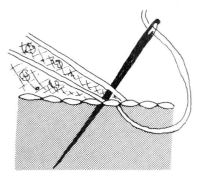

Finish here with a couple of whipping stitches. Ensure both ends of the lace meet leaving the tails free for joining

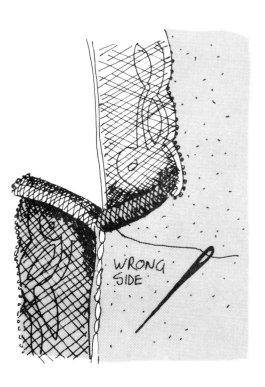

A Casing for Ribbon

About 2 cm (¾ in) up from the lace edge on the sleeve on the fold pierce a hole with a stiletto and work an eyelet. Measure a piece of insertion lace to fit inside the sleeve. Join the lace with a small seam. Place the raw edges of the seam against the sleeve seam, WRONG sides together, centring the eyelet in the middle of the insertion. Tack the lace in place through the middle of the insertion all round the sleeve. If using a non-transparent fabric, carefully tack along both sides of the insertion on the wrong side. On the right side, the tacking can be used as a guide for the feather stitching.

Feather Stitch

Thread a no. 9 crewel needle with two strands of stranded cotton approximately 1 m (1 yd) long. Secure the thread at the sleeve seam with a backstitch just above the insertion, and on the right side of work commence feather stitching. Holding the work with your left hand in the sleeve opening near the lace and working towards you, place your thumb on the thread so that it lies directly along line of insertion visible through the voile sleeve. Place the needle in at A and bring it out at B (through all thicknesses of material and lace) with the thread around the needle and pull it through. Again place your left thumb on the thread, guiding it down the line of insertion, swing the thread above to the left of your thumb this time and take another small stitch angling it in towards centre thread. Continue in this manner right around the sleeve stitching through the voile and insertion. Work the other edge of insertion the same way, thereby forming a casing for the ribbon.

On the sewing machine, gather the neck edge along the gathering line from hemstitch to hemstitch and draw the threads up so the neck measures 29 cm (11½ in) or the length required. Take the measurement from the centre of one band to the centre of the other band (i.e. centre front to centre front).

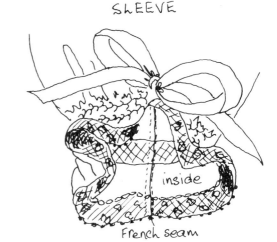

SLEEVE

French seam

inside

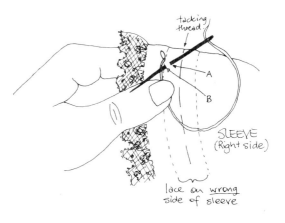

tacking thread

A

B

SLEEVE (Right side)

lace on wrong side of sleeve

FEATHER STITCHING.

To finish the neck edge, turn one long edge of bias strip under 5 mm (¼ in), press. Pin the raw edge of the bias strip to neck, right sides together, extending the bias 5 mm (¼ in) beyond the edge of each front band.

Machine stitch the binding to the neck edge between the two rows of gathering stitches. Trim to 3 mm (1/8 in). Turn the extended end of the bias to the inside. Fold the bias to the inside, placing the pressed edge over machine stitching. Slipstitch the bias binding into the machine stitching. Finish the other end to correspond. Feather stitch around this band on the right side and whip the remaining lace around the neck edge, placing the right side of the lace against the right side of the nightgown.

Blind Hemming

Turn in the raw edge of the hem 5 mm (¼ in) and fold again for 2.5 cm (1 in) and press. Commence with a few small stitches into the hem. Take the needle through one or two threads of the nightgown fabric just under the folded hem at A. Insert the needle into the hem at B. Run the point of the needle along the inside fold approximately 5 mm (¼ in) and emerge at C. Take the needle back into the fabric just below C and continue in this manner.

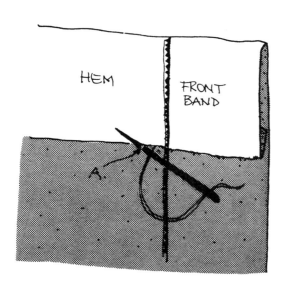

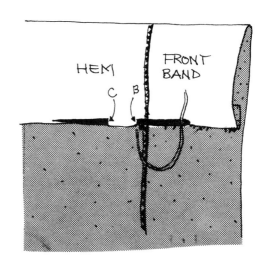

Buttonholes

Fold the band at the first buttonhole, making sure the edges of the band are even, then with sharp scissors make a small incision. Release the fold and enlarge the incision at the top and bottom until it will accommodate the button.

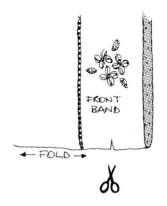

Using a no. 9 crewel needle threaded with machine cotton, overcast the edge of the buttonhole, taking the needle three threads into fabric. Once you reach the starting point again, commence buttonholing. The needle goes in through the opening and out just below the overcasting. The thread from the knotted edge should pass behind the needle and pass under its point in a clockwise circle. When pulling the thread through, pull it back towards the cut edge. At each end of the buttonhole, work one diagonal stitch, one straight stitch and one diagonal stitch. To end off, take the needle to the back of the work, and slip it through the back of the stitches and cut the thread.

Sew the buttons on to correspond with buttonholes.

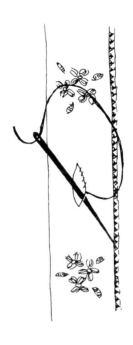

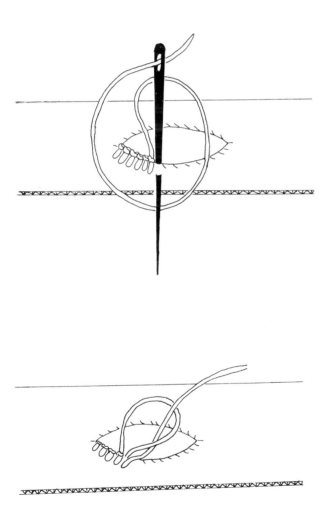

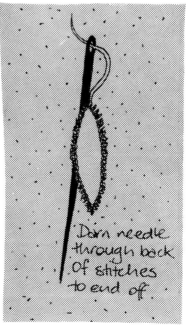

Darn needle through back of stitches to end off.

5 Crib Blanket

Materials

Woollen crib blanket
80 cm (7/8 yd) x 115 cm (45 in) Cashmilon lining
No. 18 chenille needle
Tailors chalk
DMC tapestry wool. Suggested colours:
  Roses 7950, 7121, 7191
  Lavender 7241
  Long, middle, shortest daisy trail 7194, 7121, 7191
  Petals and centres of forget-me-nots 7800, 7745
  Leaves 7402

Wool embroidery is very satisfying and seems to be a favourite for many people as it grows quickly, is easy to handle and, best of all, is not too taxing on the eyes.

In creating your design, one basic rule should be observed. Consider firstly where the design is to be placed. For example, if you are working a crib blanket, which is to be tucked in round the bottom and sides of a cot with a sheet folded back over the top section, it would be pointless to embroider the edges, as none of the embroidery would be visible when the blanket is in use. Having selected the area to be embroidered and the threads to be used, decide where you want the focal point to be.

New Stitches and Techniques

Wool rose
Lavender
French knots
Fly stitch
Forget-me-nots
Fibrone rose

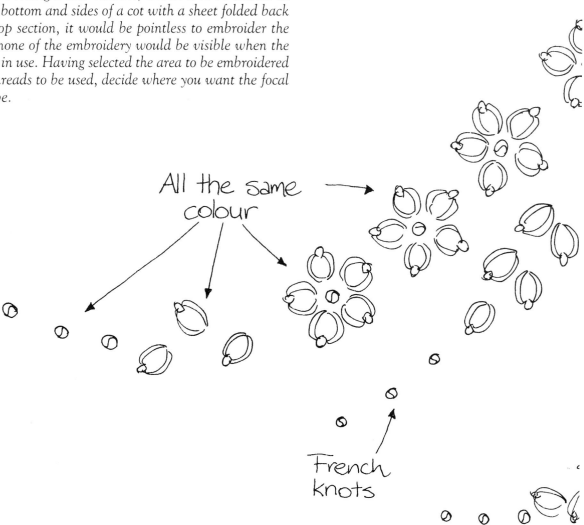

All the same colour

French knots

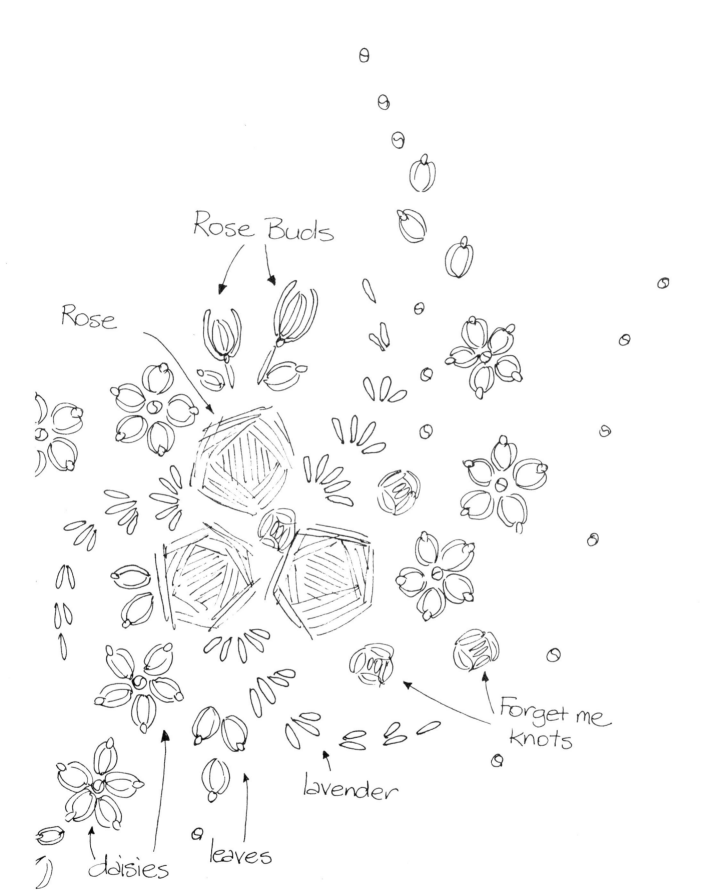

Rose Buds

Rose

Forget me
knots

lavender

leaves

daisies

On the crib blanket, centre a dinner plate and tack a line around the outside in coloured machine cotton, marking the circumference of the circle at five equidistant points. Each of these points will be the centre of a spray of flowers, so that every flower and leaf will radiate out from the centre in curved lines forming a harmonious pattern. (As in flower arranging, it is always better to work with odd numbers.) First the roses are worked, as they are the focal point of each spray, next the lavender, then daisies, forget-me-nots and buds, and lastly the leaves, so that one is working from the inside of the spray to the outside.

Roses

Select three graduating shades of coloured wool in which to work the roses and thread a no. 18 chenille needle with a length of the deepest shade. Select one of the five points on your tacked circle and, using the tailors chalk, mark three radiating lines, about 1.5 cm (5/8 in) in the middle. Note that one chalk line is on the inside of the tacked circle, and the other two lines are on the outside. (Note also that the colours used in the diagrams have been chosen to make the groups of stitches clear and are not intended as a guide for you to use.)

To Begin a Rose

Work a square in satin stitch over these chalk lines, slanting the stitches so that they radiate out from the middle of the design. Commence a square by placing the needle in at A and bringing it out at B, leaving a tail, which will darn in as you continue. Satin stitch to both sides of the line, padding the stitches and forming a square. There should be about five or six stitches on the bottom layer and four or five in the top layer of padding. Take the last stitch to the back of the work. The group of roses may all be worked at the same time by carrying the thread across on the wrong wide of the work, but be extra careful not to pull the connecting threads or the material will pucker. To finish off the thread on the back of the work, take the point of the needle through the thread at the base and then darn it back and forth, splitting the wool with the needle each time. Once or twice is enough.

On the diagrams I have marked each corner of the square to help you follow the construction of the rose, but you won't need these once you have mastered the technique. When placing the woollen threads in and out of the fabric, be sure to leave enough room for the threads to lie neatly alongside each other – in other words allow for the thickness of the threads.

Second Round

Thread the needle with the second shade of wool. A knot in the end is permissible or begin by darning the thread into the back of the work to secure it and bring the point of the needle out at a corner of the completed square at point A. Working anti-clockwise around the

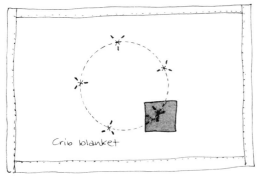

Crib blanket

DETAIL OF INSET FROM FIGURE 1

1.5 cm chalk line

tacking thread

1.5 cm chalk line

1.5 cm chalk line

Design radiates from this point

1.5 cm   1.5 cm

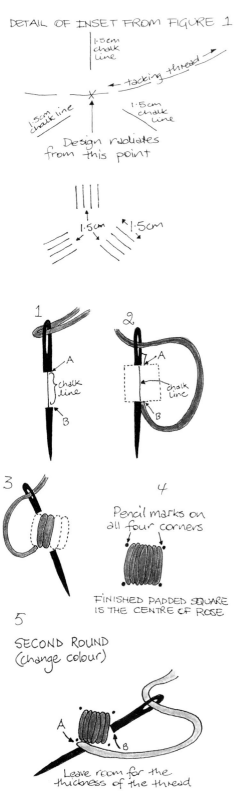

1

A

chalk line

B

2

A

chalk line

B

3

4

Pencil marks on all four corners

FINISHED PADDED SQUARE IS THE CENTRE OF ROSE

5

SECOND ROUND (change colour)

A

B

Leave room for the thickness of the thread

42

rose, put the needle back in at B and bring it out again just below A, guiding the thread into place around the base of the square and keeping the tension quite firm — otherwise the second round tends to work its way up and over the first square, obscuring the centre. The needle is then placed just below B a second time and brought out again just below the last thread at A. The third time the needle is put in just below B and emerges at the pencil dot at C. The same three steps are repeated, this time between C and D, finally emerging at the next pencil dot at E. Work four sides in this manner, always working from a corner of the initial square to a middle section of the next side. This procedure has simply squared off the initial square. Turn your work as you complete each side. Complete the rest of the roses with this second round and end off.

Third Round
Thread the needle with the palest shade of wool. Forget all the steps from the previous round and secure the thread in the back of the work and bring the needle up at A. Work two stitches across to point B, bringing the needle up at C, down at D, and up at E. Work two rows straight up the sides of the rose, extending a little beyond the corner. Continue in this manner.

To achieve a more interesting appearance, occasionally cross one stitch over the other to give a slightly irregular appearance, until you have worked five sides to the rose. You may think your finished rose looks irregular and disorderly, but this is the character of the rose.

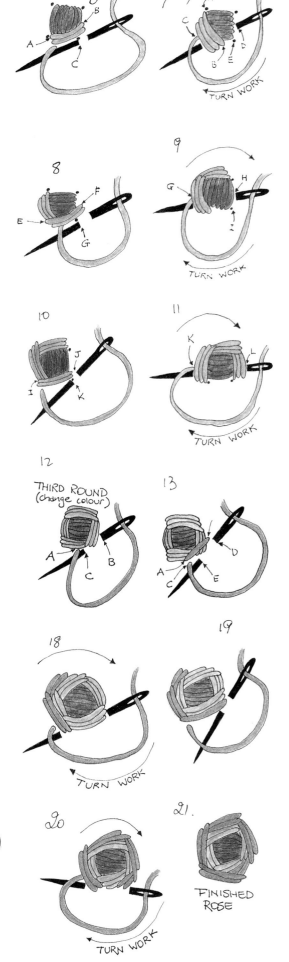

43

Lavender

Thread the needle with your selected wool, secure it in at the back of a rose and bring the needle to the front of the work at the base of the lavender. Working the first straight stitch along the line, bring the needle back almost to the same point just a little lower than the base of the first stitch. Fan the short straight stitches out at the top, keeping the bases of the stitches close together in small semi-circle. Five stitches is a good number to begin with. As you work up the stem of lavender, reduce the number of petals by one each time, dropping the excess petal on the outside curve. Each time a group of stitches is completed, move back to the line and work the first stitch along the line. Leave a small gap between groups. This gives the illusion of a stalk running through the middle.

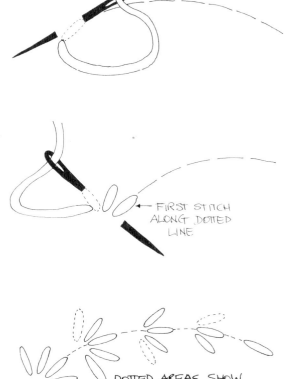

FIRST STITCH ALONG DOTTED LINE

DOTTED AREAS SHOW PETALS THAT SHOULD BE DROPPED

Daisies

Thread the needle with your selected colour, secure the end in at the back of the work, emerging about 1 cm (3/8 in) along the line to be worked. The first lazy daisy petal is worked along the line towards the rose; the second petal at right angles to the first (leaving a gap in the centre of the daisy); and the third petal with the base opposite the first but angled up slightly, which makes room for the fourth and fifth petals – the petals are at 12, 2, 4, 7 and 9 o'clock. Work the required number of daisies down the line, trying to angle the petals so they inter-lock with each other. Finish the line of daisies with a few single petals (with the base of each petal on the line) and finish with french knots. This prevents the blunt appearance that would result if the daisies were to end abruptly. Centres are worked in french knots.

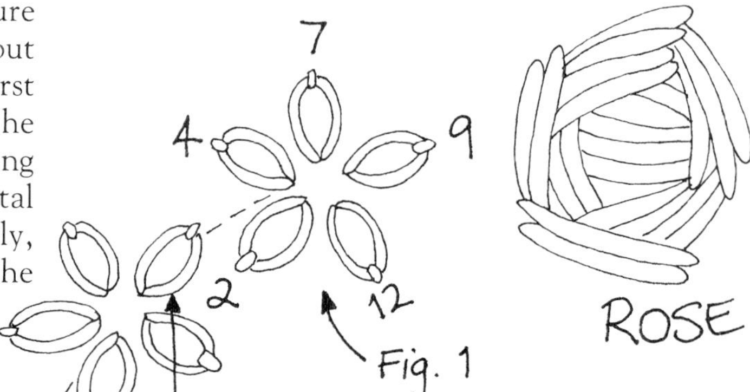

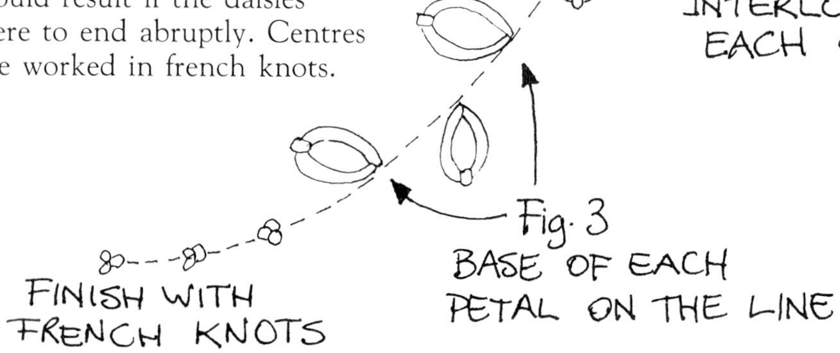

7
4
9
2
12
Fig. 1

ROSE

Fig. 2
ANGLE PETALS TO
INTERLOCK WITH
EACH OTHER

Fig. 3
BASE OF EACH
PETAL ON THE LINE

FINISH WITH
FRENCH KNOTS

French Knots

The needle and thread are brought to the front of the
work at A. The needle is held in your right hand and
the thread in your left hand. Wind the thread clockwise
around the needle once only with your left hand. Put
the point of the needle back down into the fabric at B,
just next to the starting point at A (if it goes into the
same hole the knot will pull straight through to the
back). The knot must be in place on the fabric before
the thread is pulled through. French knots may have
more than one twist of thread on the needle, but one
is sufficient when you are working with wool.

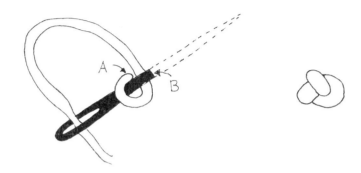

Forget-me-nots

Thread the needle with the selected thread and
commence by working two stitches on each side of a
square going in and out of the same holes. Work the
centre in the same manner, with just two stitches. If
working a group of these little flowers, try angling them
differently to achieve a slightly irregular effect.

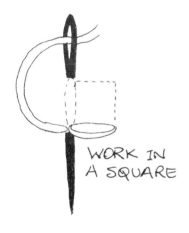

WORK IN
A SQUARE

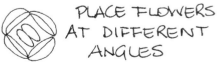

PLACE FLOWERS
AT DIFFERENT
ANGLES

Buds and Leaves

Buds are worked in the dark or middle shade of the rose colour. Make three straight stitches about 1 cm (3/8 in) long into the same holes at the top and bottom, angling the base of each bud so they look as though they belong to the roses.

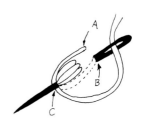

The stalk and calyx of the rose are worked in green in fly stitch around the bud. Bring the needle up beyond the bud at A, hold the thread at the base of the bud, put the needle in at B and bring it up at C, keeping the thread around the needle at C. Then push the needle in at D to form a small stalk to bud.

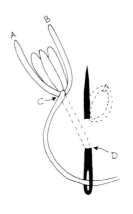

Work a leaf beside the bud in lazy daisy and continue to work leaves around the spray of flowers in groups of three or five, adding a french knot here and there for effect. The leaves are worked in groups of three and five by working them in a V so that the base of the V points towards the centre of the spray. This creates the illusion of a twig connecting the spray to the roses or daisies.

The designs and variations for using these stitches are endless – plates, books, pictures, photos, your garden all offer inspiration. Remember, no flowers are identical so there is no need to strive for absolute accuracy – your creation should have a personal flavour. Threads may also be varied to create different textures. Perle cottons add a lighter touch and silk threads are a possibility too. For example, work the daisy in wool, and do the straight stitch in perle or silk thread. Different colours also extend the possibilities.

Lining

Stretch the blanket, right side down, on a table or on the floor and smooth it out. Pin and tack a lining (a Cashmilon and wool mixture is a good weight), with the raw edges folded under, to under the edge of the blanket's satin binding. Blind hem the lining into place.

Fibrone Rose

This is a very simple and quick method of making roses and a very effective one. Fibrone roses may also be used as an alternative to wool roses. Using a thread of tapestry wool and a no. 18 chenille needle, commence by making a well padded satin stitch centre. Select a lighter colour wool and work round the centre in stem stitch, loosely at first, so that the stitches lie close to the top of the centre, then gradually make the stitches tighter and tighter until the last stitches lie close to fabric. Keeping the thread to the left of the needle, bring the needle back each time half way to the starting point of the last stitch.

wool

Perle cotton

FIBRONE
ROSE

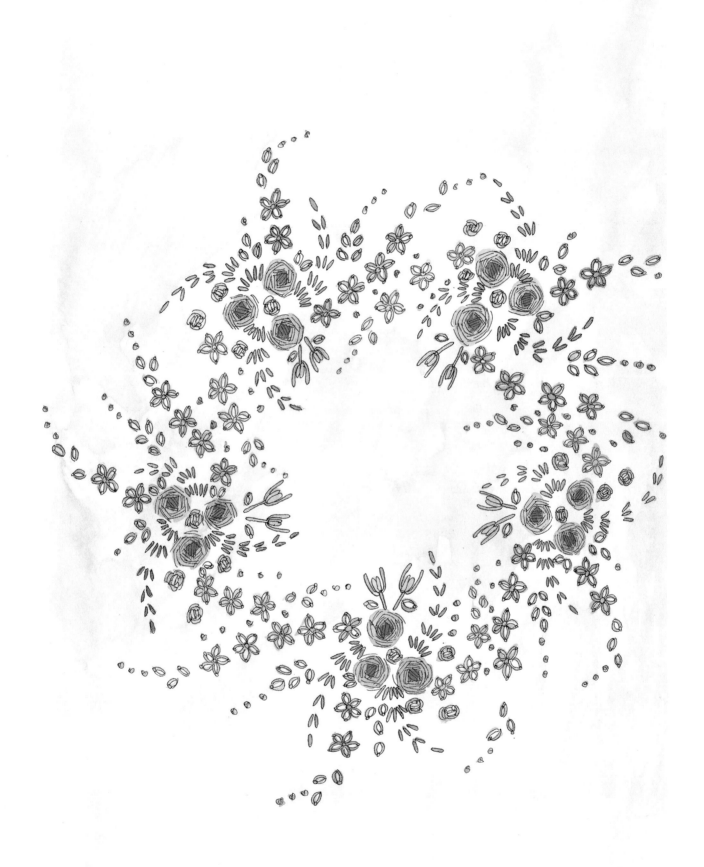

6 Lily of the Valley Pillow Slip

Materials

33 cm (13 in) x 94 cm (37 in) cotton voile
3 m (3 3/8 yds) x 5 cm (2 in) lace edging
Stranded cottons: white, green
No. 9 crewel needle
Water-soluble fabric marking pen
30 cm (12 in) x 40 cm (16 in) pillow
Optional satin underslip: 33 cm (12½ in) x 94 cm (37 in) satin

Small pillows are both useful and decorative. They make a lovely gift for someone in hospital, are a great comfort to tuck under one's head when reading in bed, and they look wonderful scattered on a bed.

Before cutting the fabric, draw a thread to ensure the threads are running straight, and cut along the drawn thread line. Trim one selvedge edge from the voile and fold that short end to the wrong side and turn under a flap measuring approximately 13 cm (5 in). Fold the fabric again, wrong sides together, so that the selvedge lies 5 mm (¼ in) beyond the first fold. Trim the second selvedge. The flap should be on the upper right hand side. The distance between the two folds should measure 40 cm (16 in). Press the folds in place and mark the folds with a line of tacking to save having to measure all over again later.

To place the lines of drawn thread work, measure in 4 cm (1½ in) from the top of the left-hand fold and mark with a pin. Still on the left-hand side, measure down from the top 5.5 cm (2¼ in) and where this point meets the one measured in from the left mark a dot with the water-soluble pen. This is dot A. (The 5.5 cm or 2¼ in, includes a 1.5 cm (5/8 in) seam allowance at the top, which is not necessary when measuring from the folded edge.) Measure 16 cm (6½ in) from dot A parallel with the top edge of the fabric and mark in dot B. Measure from dot A parallel with the shorter folded left hand edge of the pillow slip and mark in dot C. These form the points between which you will draw threads.

New Stitches and Techniques

Lily of the valley flowers
Zigzag hemstitch
Gathering and simultaneous application of lace (Method 2)

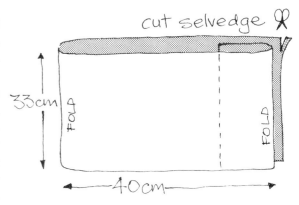

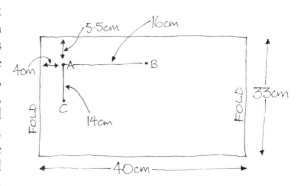

Drawn Thread Work

Drawing threads in the middle of the fabric requires a little patience and care, as the thread must not be pulled beyond the given points. It may be best to first practice the technique on a scrap of fabric. If you were working in a heavier fabric, such as linen, the pulled threads would be eased out of the fabric back to given points, re-threaded through a needle and carefully darned back into the fabric to strengthen the ends. The voile is so fine this not feasible, so here is my method for extracting threads. With a fine needle or pin select a thread approximately 2 cm (¾ in) from dot A along the line to be drawn and ease the thread out of the fabric, taking great care not to draw the thread past A. Snip this thread and gently ease the longest thread towards dot B, stopping gathers approximately 2 cm (¾ in) from B. To snap the thread, gather together a nice little bundle of gathers and hold in both hands. With the index finger of each hand under the fabric and your thumbs on top pressed hard together, quickly jerk your left hand over your right thumb to snap the thread. Draw the snapped thread from the fabric and ease out the remaining ends of thread back to dot A and dot B. Second and subsequent threads are drawn from the middle and towards dots A and B. Ease them out one at a time from the centre of the line, drawing out as much thread as possible without extending between the given points. Cut the withdrawn thread close to fabric. This only leaves you with a small amount of thread to extract from both ends. Draw nine threads all together from A to B and from A to C. A small hole or gap in the threads will appear in the corner — this is normal. Commencing at dot B on the lower edge of the drawn thread line, work a line of hemstitch (see baby's nightgown) turning the corner at A and working towards C. Keep the bundles of thread picked up by the needle quite small so that the work will not pucker when the second row is completed. When you reach dot C, overcast the end very gently as there is nothing much to hold those threads in place. Use the same method when overcasting the small hole at A.

From point C hemstitch along the opposite side of the drawn threads, but this time divide the original bundles in half, binding half of one bundle to half of the next bundle. This will give a crisscross effect. To end off the cotton, take the needle to the back of the work and darn the thread back through the stitches.

Work a second row of drawn thread work in the same manner 2 cm (¾ in) inside the first two rows. This forms a frame for the embroidery. Make the second frame approximately 1 cm (3/8 in) shorter than the first frame at each end.

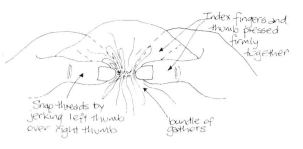

Index fingers and thumb pressed firmly together

Snap threads by jerking left thumb over right thumb

bundle of gathers

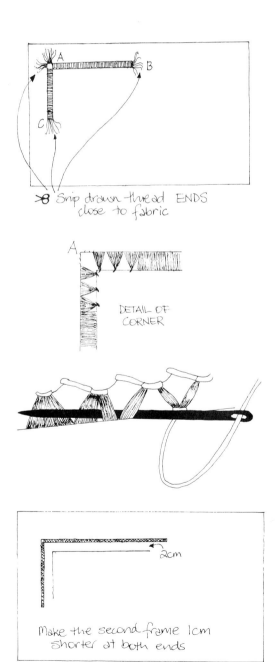

Snip drawn thread ENDS close to fabric

DETAIL OF CORNER

Make the second frame 1cm shorter at both ends

2cm

49

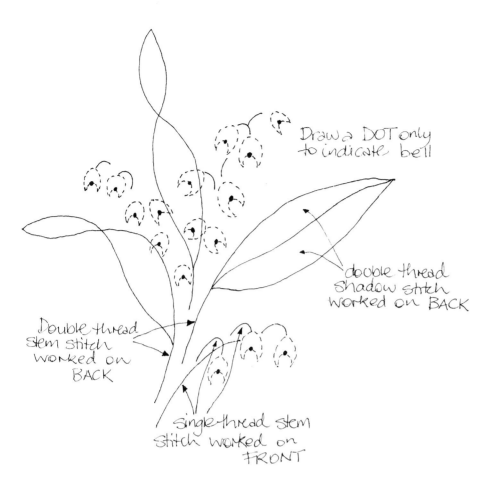

Draw a DOT only to indicate bell

double thread shadow stitch worked on BACK

Double thread stem stitch worked on BACK

single-thread stem stitch worked on FRONT

Trace the lily of the valley design into the corner but do not draw in the flowers; it is easier to embroider them if a dot is made instead of the flower.

Leaves

Use two strands of green stranded cotton and a no. 9 crewel needle and work on the wrong side of the fabric. Commence stem stitching at the bottom of the leaf stem, but connect the stitches so they will look like back stitch on the front of work. This gives continuity with the shadow stitch of the leaf. Where a leaf has a division down the middle, shadow stitch up the right side of the division, then turn your work and shadow stitch down the other side of the leaf, picking up the centre stitches only instead of fabric down the vein of the leaf. The leaves need to be embroidered before the flowers as some of the flowers are embroidered over the top of the leaves. •Stems are embroidered in one strand of cotton on the right side of the work.

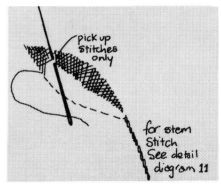

pick up stitches only

for stem stitch see detail diagram 11

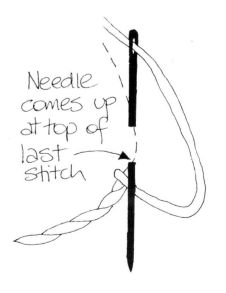

Needle comes up at top of last stitch

Flowers

Use a no. 9 crewel needle and two strands of white stranded cotton. When embroidering the flowers, hold your work so that the head of the bell is closest to you. The shape and size of each bell to be worked can be seen on the transfer pattern above. Do not draw in the bell but follow the diagrams, making your first stitch approximately 4 mm (1/8 in) long, or the distance between the dot and the imagined head of bell.

1. Place the needle into the dot bringing the point out towards you.
2. Work three satin stitches side by side and, when bringing the needle up for the fourth stitch, begin shaping the head of the bell by emerging just short of the previous stitches.
3. Using the thread as a guide to shape the bell, make the next stitch a little longer and curve it in slightly.
4. Repeat step 3, but this time make the stitch longer again and slightly curved.
5. Bring the needle out at the head of the bell and pad three more stitches back over first three stitches. Half the bell is now complete.
6. To complete the other half of the bell work only two more satin stitches in the middle before shaping the second side to correspond with the first. Pad over the last two stitches in the middle before finishing off behind by darning the thread through the back of the flowers.

When the embroidery is completed, roll and whip both the short raw edges of the fabric to the wrong side.

To Make Up

To make up the pillow slip, fold along the original creases, which you have marked with tacking, WRONG sides together and sew about 1 cm (3/8 in) in from the raw edge along the seam lines. Trim back to about 2 mm (1/16 in) and turn the pillow slip inside out. Now fold the flap once more before completing the second row of stitching of the french seam (right sides together). This method will hide the finished seam when the pillow slip is turned right side out. Turn right side out.

HEAD OF BELL

use the thread as a guide for the shape of the bell

pad three stitches over these stitches

Finished bell showing five padded satin stitches in the centre

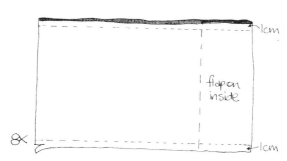

1cm

flap on inside

1cm

To Whip and Gather the Lace

Before commencing, measure the half-way point on the lace as a guide by which to gauge how full to make the gathering of the lace.

Commence whipping the lace onto the pillow slip at one of the bottom corners and leave about 2 cm (¾ in) of lace for joining. Place the right side of the lace to the right side of the pillow slip. Secure the lace to the corner with three small satin stitches. Run the needle through the seam for about 1 mm (1/16 in) and, when emerging, bring the needle up about 4 mm (1/8 in) ahead into the lace. As the thread is pulled tight, the lace will form a small loop. Secure this loop with another stitch over the point where the thread emerges through the fabric and lace, leaving the loop free. Continue in this manner, for about four stitches to allow a little more fullness in the lace at the corners, then lengthen the stitch in the fabric to 4 mm (1/8 in) until the next corner is almost reached, when you should reduce the stitches in the fabric to 1 mm (1/16 in) to give more fullness at the corner. Continue in this manner until you have completed all sides of the pillow slip, including the top part only over the opening.

If you join the lace a little way from the corner, a pleat can then be worked in the lace at the corner to hide the join.

The finished appearance of the pillow will be greatly enhanced by making a white satin underslip. Make it the same size as the lily of the valley pillow slip and follow its instructions for making up.

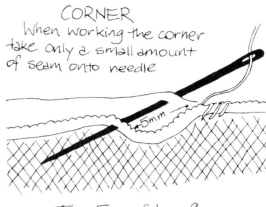

CORNER
When working the corner take only a small amount of seam onto needle

5mm

Take 5mm of lace for corner

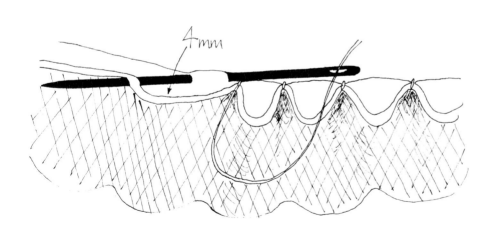

4mm

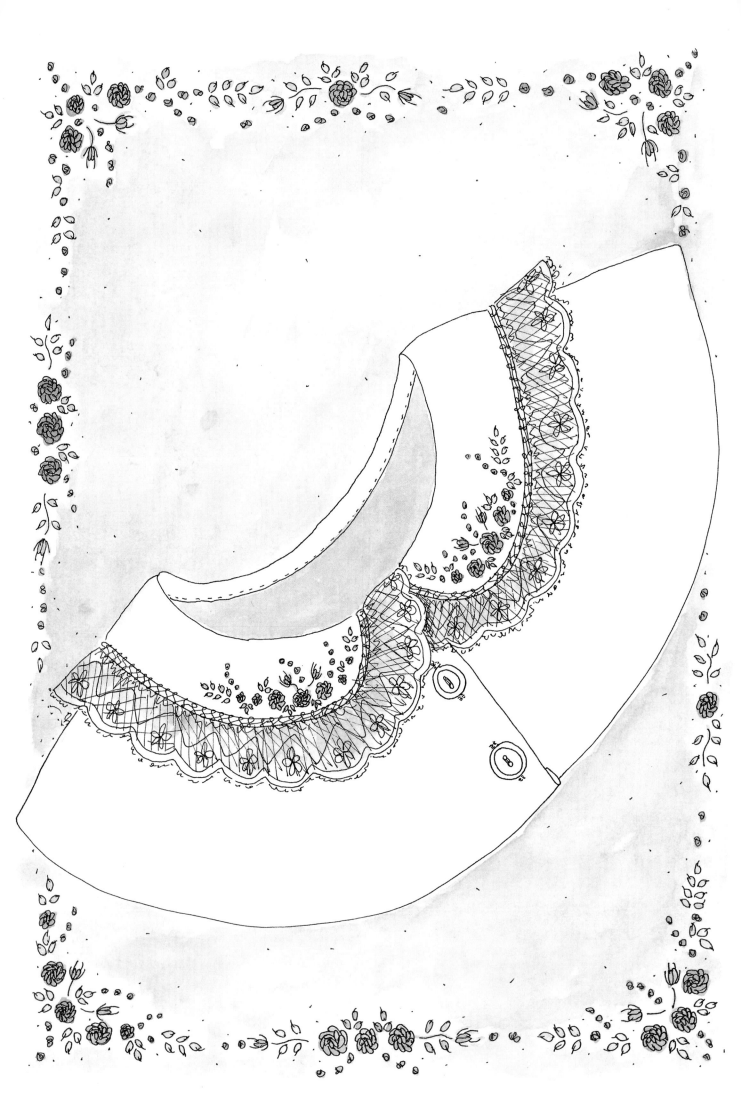

7 Collars

Materials

50 cm (20 in) x 115 cm (45 in) cotton voile
1 m (1¼ yds) x 2.5 cm (1 in) lace edging
3 small buttons or press studs
Stranded cottons: grub rose collar – three shades of one colour for rose, one colour for leaves
daisy collar – one colour (or more) for flowers and one colour for leaves
No. 9 crewel needle, no. 9 straw needle
Sheet of paper 35 cm (14 in) x 40 cm (16 in)
Water-soluble fabric marking pen

These false collars have been a great success with my students, who enjoy making and wearing them. Choosing different colours and designs makes them all look so different. I include two different designs for embroidery here, but the possibilities are vast: you could use your friend's initials, if you are giving it as a gift, some simple daisies, or even just coloured spots.

New Stitches and Techniques

Small bullion (grub) roses and buds
Smocking knot
Satin stitch flowers
Satin stitch leaves
(Method 2)
Faggoting

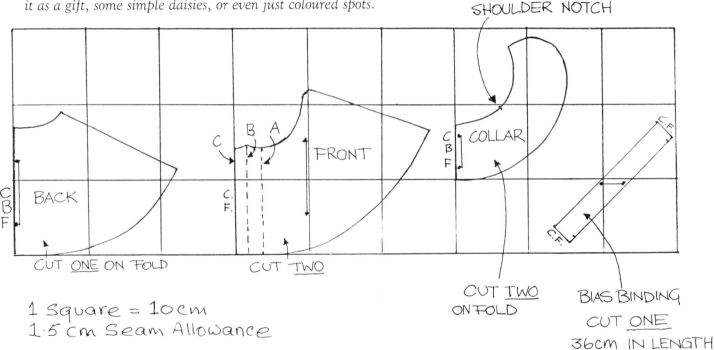

1 Square = 10 cm
1.5 cm Seam Allowance

Applying the Design

One thing to remember is that, when you apply the design to the voile, you must make sure it doesn't extend over the seam allowances. Dot in the seam allowance first and then place the design. Draw the design onto one section of the collar only. Draw one end first then turn the collar over to the reverse side to trace the other end – as the fabric is sheer the marking will show through. Your drawing will be on opposite sides of the fabric so you must take care to embroider both ends on the same side.

Bullion Rose Design

Work the bullion roses using the same method used on the face washer, but this time use a single thread of stranded cotton and a no. 9 straw needle. Instead of working a bullion centre, a padded satin stitch centre is used here. Keep it very small — approximately 1 mm (1/16 in) — and work six or seven satin stitches in the darkest shade. Next work the first round in the second shade using about eight or nine twists on the needle and taking four to five bullions to complete the circle. Finally, work the last round in the palest shade. The largest rose takes about seven bullions to complete the circle; the two smaller roses on each side would be completed with five bullions, and the tiny roses on the edge would only have one round in the second shade.

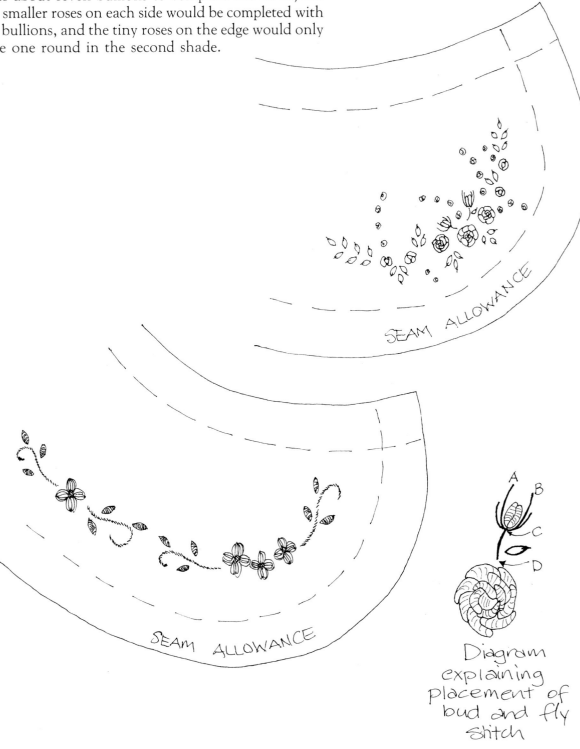

SEAM ALLOWANCE

SEAM ALLOWANCE

Diagram explaining placement of bud and fly stitch

56

Buds are worked by placing two small bullion stitches side by side in any of the three shades you choose; I chose the second shade here. So that the buds look as though they belong to the roses, ensure that the base of each bud is angled towards the rose. The green fly stitch around the buds is worked in single thread by bringing the needle up at A, holding the thread near the base of the bullion, pushing the needle down at B and up again at C with the thread around the needle. Repeat this step, making the second fly stitch slightly smaller and wider when emerging at C the second time. Use the thread to form the stalk of the bud by taking it straight into D. A small leaf can then be worked to one side of the stem in lazy daisy stitch. The rest of the leaves are worked in lazy daisy stitch and, as there is really nothing much to attach the thread to at the back of the work, a small knot is permissible.

To end off I find a smocking knot is very handy when there are only one or two threads to end off into. If using the knot, pick up one or two threads with your needle on the back of the work, bring the needle through the loop, then bring the needle back through the second loop formed while taking the needle through the first loop, this forms a figure 8 knot and is quite secure.

The french knots are scattered about and it is advisable to work them in a pale colour, as the thread is continued behind from one to the other in a line and the thread would be quite obvious through the sheer fabric if you used a dark shade. Work french knots with two or three twists around the needle.

Satin Stitch Flower Design

When tracing the design, just use dots for the petals and centres with a small stroke for leaves. Embroidery petals will be worked to both sides of the dot. Each flower is worked in a single thread of stranded cotton using a no. 9 crewel needle. There are about sixteen to eighteen stitches in each petal.

To commence the petal, hold your work so that the centre of the flower to be worked is between you and the petal you will be working on. Place the needle in at the top of the petal with the point of needle coming towards you and work three small base stitches side by side. I always begin in the centre and work one stitch to either side. Then bring the needle up in the centre hole and continue the rest of the fifteen stitches in the same two holes top and bottom, using your thumb to spread the stitches to left and right and guiding the thread into place. The petals grow considerably in size from the initial three base stitches, so bear this in mind when starting each new petal and allowing 1 mm (1/16 in) extra for this expansion so that you leave room in the middle for a centre. The centre is also worked in satin stitch (about nine or ten stitches).

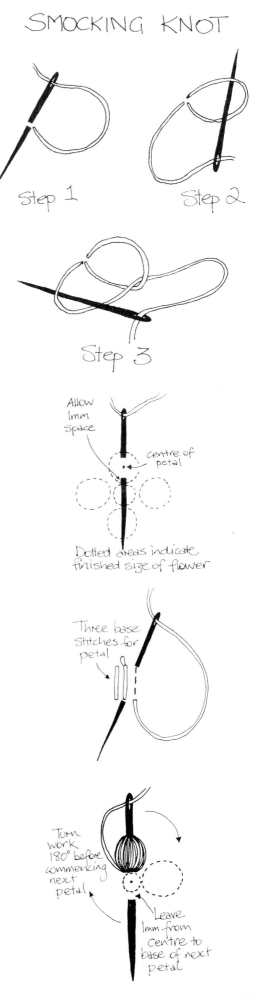

SMOCKING KNOT

Step 1

Step 2

Step 3

Allow 1mm space

centre of petal

Dotted areas indicate finished size of flower

Three base stitches for petal

Turn work 180° before commencing next petal

Leave 1mm from centre to base of next petal

Satin Stitch Leaves Method No. 2

The leaves and stems are worked in a single thread of stranded cotton with a no. 9 crewel needle. Commence stem stitch from the flowers and work towards the end of spray, then take the needle to the back of the work and darn back down through the stitches behind until you are level with the first leaf to be worked. Bring the needle to the front of the work at the base of a leaf and make four or five satin stitches the length of the leaf in and out of the same two holes top and bottom (this forms the padding). Bring the needle out at the base of the leaf, taking the first satin stitch half way up the right hand side to form an angle. When you bring the needle up on the left side, begin the shaping. The first three stitches are used to shape the leaf on the left-hand side only – follow the dotted line in the diagram; the right side is perfectly straight, just continue up the side of the padding stitches. Once you have shaped the first three or four stitches on the left, commence working and shaping stitches back in towards the point of the leaf. When the point of the leaf is reached, take the needle through the padding stitches only, which will give you a nice sharp point. Each leaf should be finished off separately. Then commence each new leaf with a small running stitch from the tip of the leaf towards the base and then pad with satin stitches.

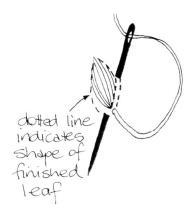

dotted line indicates shape of finished leaf

Take needle ONCE only through padding stitches

Faggoting or Twisted Insertion Stitch

Once the embroidery is completed, the water-soluble pen markings are rinsed away in cold running water, the fabric pressed, and the two pieces of the collar machine stitched together around the seam allowance, with RIGHT sides together. The seam allowance is trimmed to about 3 mm (1/8 in) and the corners should be snipped. Turn the collar right side out and press.

The collar is then tacked in the centre of a piece of paper, running the tacking close to the outer edge of the collar. If you are using a good French or Swiss lace, you will find a thread running through the straight edge which, if pulled gently, will gather the lace. If there is no thread to gather, use a fine running stitch close to the top of the lace for gathering. Mark the half way point on the lace and gently draw up the gathering thread, working towards the middle from both ends. Ease out the gathers so that the lace is only very slightly gathered. More fullness will be required around the curves at the

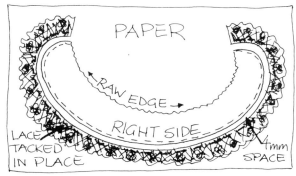

PAPER

RAW EDGE

RIGHT SIDE

LACE TACKED IN PLACE

4mm SPACE

front of the collar. Commence pinning the lace to the paper at centre back, about 4 mm (1/8 in) from the edge of the collar. This step is quite tedious but it is worth being patient and getting the gathers of the lace and its distance from the collar even. Ensure the lace is full enough round the curve so that it doesn't drag at the edge. When the lace is pinned to your satisfaction, tack it in place on the paper along the straight edge of the lace.

Take two long strands of embroidery thread in your selected colour and commence faggoting. Secure the thread into the edge of the collar; keeping the thread to the right hand side, take the needle through the edge of the lace from the front to the back and up and over the thread. This feels quite awkward at first, as you feel as though you are sewing backwards. Next, still keeping the thread to the right side, take a stitch through the edge of the collar from the right side to the wrong side and, keeping the point of the needle over the top of the thread, pull. The needle must always enter the fabric and lace from the right side and there are no short cuts—the thread must be pulled through each time. This is such a rewarding stitch that once you get into the swing of it, it becomes really enjoyable to work. Keep the stitches about 3 mm (1/8 in) apart along the edge of the collar, and, when rounding the corners, very slightly condense the stitches on the collar and extend them in the lace, so the stitches remain alternate. When faggoting is completed, remove the tacking from the collar and lace and then make up the collar.

Making Up the Collar

Sew the shoulder seams of the back and front yokes together with french or overlocked seams. Pin the collar to the neck edge of the yoke, matching the centre back and shoulder seams with notches on the collar—the WRONG side of the collar is pinned to the RIGHT side of the yoke. Line up the edge of the lace on the collar to line A on yoke. If it doesn't quite fit, ease the yoke to fit the collar. Fold yoke front wrong sides together along line B. Now fold the fronts back along line A, right sides together, and pin over the top of lace. Take the bias strip and pin it along the neck edge. The bias strip finishes half way across the front band (i.e. centre front. Tack through all the layers along the seam line, then machine sew right around the neck edge on the seam line. Trim the seam allowance and clip the curves. Turn the front band right side out. Double fold and pin the bias strip around neck edge on the wrong side and machine sew, or hem. Make a small double hem on the lower edge of the yoke and sew it by hand or machine. Buttonholes may be worked by hand or machine, or press studs may be used instead of buttons if desired, as they will not be visible under a crew-neck sweater.

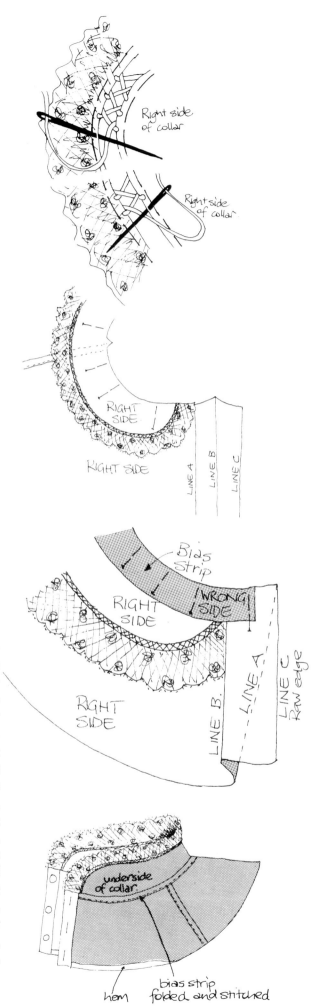

8 Half Slip and Knickers

HALF SLIP

Waist Sizes
64 cm (25 in), 67 cm (26½ in), 71 cm (28 in), 76 cm (30 in)

Materials
1.8 m (2 yds) x 115 cm (45 in) voile, georgette or batiste
1.5 m (1 5/8 yds) x 5 cm (4 in) lace edging
Stranded cotton (your colour choice)
Stiletto or tailors awl
Waist measurement + 2.5cm (1 in) x 6 mm (¼ in) elastic
No. 9 crewel needle
Water-soluble fabric marking pen

The eyelet flowers worked on this half slip and knickers are used a great deal in fine embroidery and are worth persevering with. They are shown to best advantage where there is no lining behind the embroidery as the eyelet hole is clearly visible and adds an interesting dimension to the work. The petals of the flowers may also be worked as eyelets to give a lacy effect. In this case each eyelet would need to be finished off separately by darning the thread back through the stitches on the wrong side of work.

New Stitches and Techniques
Eyelet flowers

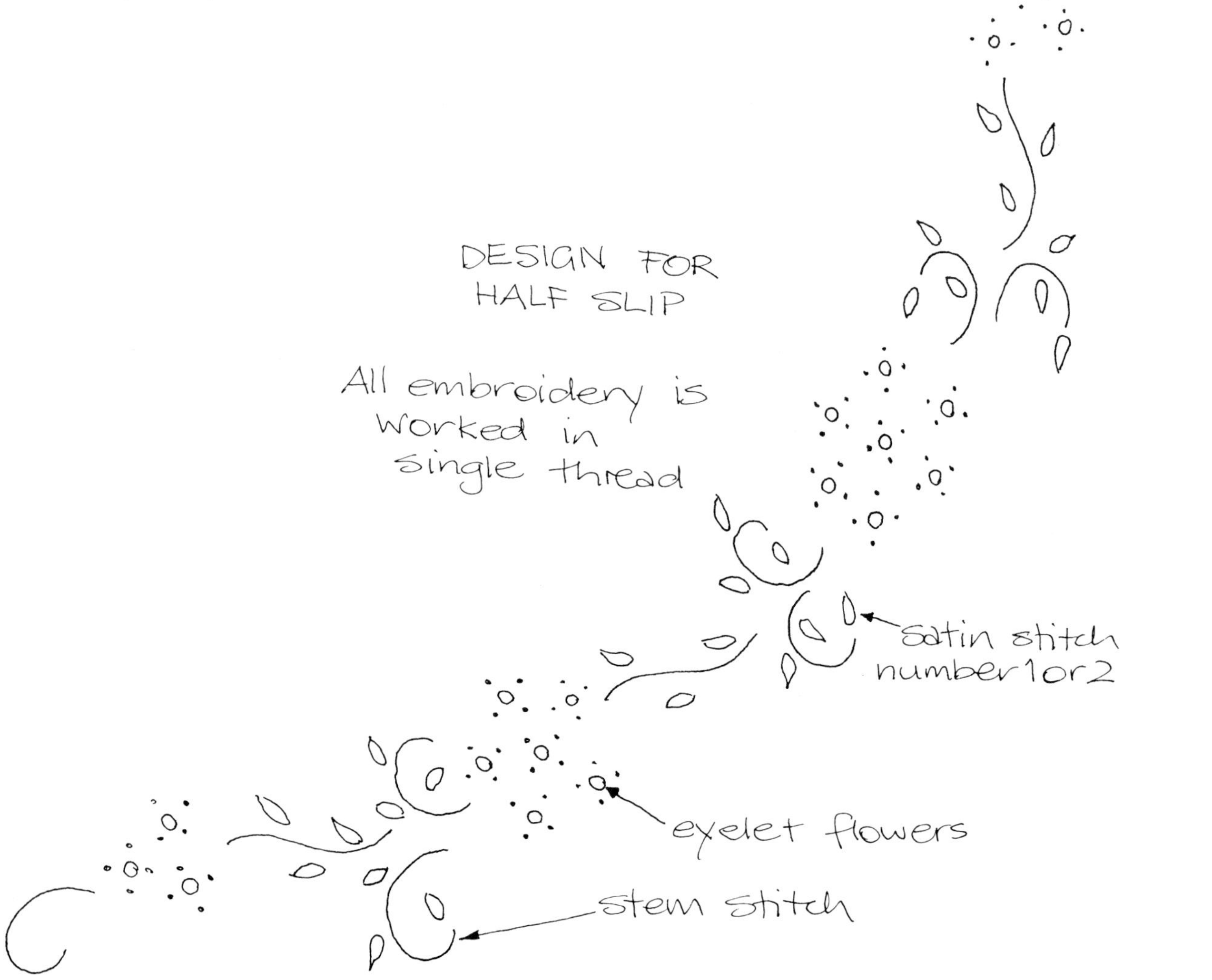

DESIGN FOR
HALF SLIP

All embroidery is
worked in
single thread

Satin stitch
number 1 or 2

eyelet flowers

stem stitch

60

Cut out the fabric and take the front section only of the half slip. Determine the centre front by folding the fabric in half lengthwise and make a crease with your thumb near the bottom. Centre your design under this crease and about 4 cm (1½ in) up from the bottom and trace it onto the fabric with a water-soluble fabric marking pen. Mark only the centres of the flowers, not the petals.

Eyelet Flowers

Using your stiletto or awl make a small hole in the fabric in the centre of the middle flower. Always begin with the centre flower so that the surrounding flowers can be moved if it becomes necessary. Use a no. 9 or 10 crewel needle with a single thread of stranded cotton and, holding the fabric across the index finger of your left hand, put the needle into the hole, emerging about 1 mm (or 1/16 in, or two or three threads) into the fabric next to the hole. Draw the thread through, leaving a small tail of cotton which will darn in with subsequent overcasting stitches.

The important points to remember when working an eyelet are:

1. to turn your work as you go so that the point of the needle is always pointing towards you as it emerges from the fabric, and
2. to keep the tension quite firm on the thread you are using.

These will ensure that the eyelet hole stays neat and round. There is no need to pack the stitches up too tightly—this will make the eyelet bulky. The thread needs to just lie next to the previous stitch not on top of it.

The eyelet is worked by overcasting the edge of the hole. Darn in the tail end of the cotton as you proceed round the hole, keeping the thread to the right of the needle. When the eyelet is completed with the last overcast stitch, bring the point of the needle up about 1 mm (less than 1/16 in) outside the eyelet to commence the first petal. If you don't allow the 1 mm (less than 1/16 in), you will run out of room before the petal is completed.

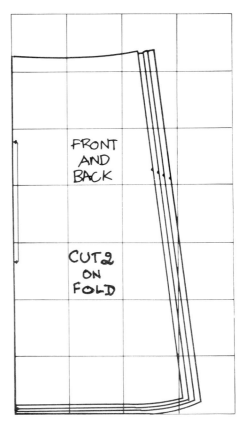

1 Square = 10 cm
1·5 cm seam allowance
Waist size
25 in 64 cm   26½ in 67 cm
28 in 71 cm   30 in 76 cm

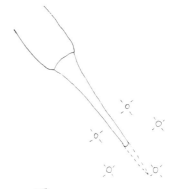

To make hole, push stiletto into fabric approx. 1·5 cm

approx. 1 mm

tail of thread is being darned in

Turn work as you go so the point of the needle is always towards you

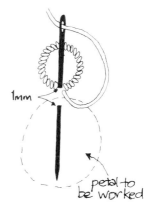

1 mm

petal to be worked

61

Now turn your work so that the eyelet is between you and the petal you are going to work on and begin the petal by placing three small stitches side by side, working the middle stitch first then one to each side. The stitches should be about 1 mm (less than 1/16 in) in size. These three stitches form the base of the petal. Now continue in satin stitch, padding up the petal by working into the same two holes at the top and bottom of the centre stitch of the petal. Make approximately sixteen stitches (including the three base stitches). As you complete each stitch, guide the thread into place with your thumb, from side to side and in the middle so the petal becomes round, raised and plump. The size of the petal will increase considerably, but it is very important to keep placing the needle into the same two holes and not let it sneak up at all, otherwise the petal will become elongated. When commencing the next petal, place it at right angles to the first, again leaving 1 mm (less than 1/16 in) between the petal and the eyelet and making the initial three stitches only about 1 mm (less than 1/16 in) long. Each flower has four petals.

Once you have completed the first flower in the group, work the other flowers around it by trying to place the first petal of each new flower into a gap between petals of the first flower. The stems are worked in stem stitch with a single thread of stranded cotton and the leaves may be worked in the same way as on the collar (project 7) or on the baby's nightgown (project 4).

Making Up the Slip

Once the embroidery is completed, sew up the side seams with very fine french seams. Make a narrow casing at the waist for elastic by turning under 5 mm (¼ in) and pressing. Turn again 1 cm (3/8 in) and machine stitch along the edge, leaving an opening near the seam to insert elastic. Run another row of machine stitching right around the top edge of the casing. Run a line of machine stitching round the very bottom edge of the slip and trim away ragged ends of fabric very close to the stitching. This will prevent the fabric from stretching while you roll and whip the lace on. Roll and whip the lace to the edge of the slip (see the method described under the baby's nightgown). Insert elastic in top casing.

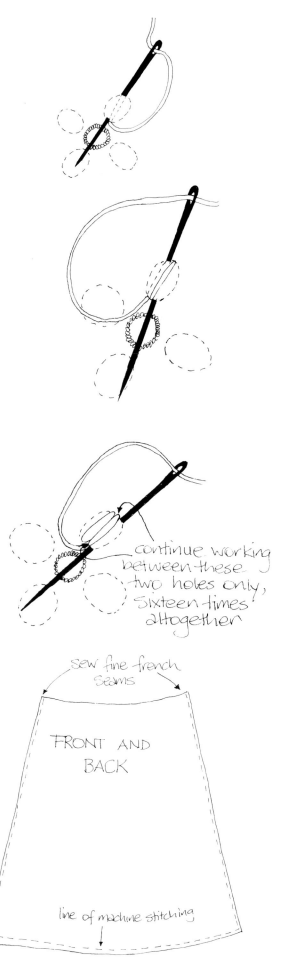

continue working between these two holes only, sixteen times altogether

sew fine french seams

FRONT AND BACK

trim back to machine stitching

line of machine stitching

Knickers

Materials

1.1 m (1 1/8 yds) x 115 cm (45 in) voile, georgette, batiste
2 m (2½ yds) x 5 cm (2 in) lace edging
Waist measurement + 2.5 cm (1 in) x 6 mm (¼ in) elastic

Cut the pieces out of the fabric and trace the design, centring it on each leg about 4 cm (1½ in) from the bottom edge of the leg. Work the design using the same method as described for the half slip. Construct the knickers as shown in the diagrams.

Finish the lower leg edges with machine stitching, as for the slip. Trim away the excess fabric and roll and whip the lace to the lower leg edges. Finish the waist edge with casing and elastic.

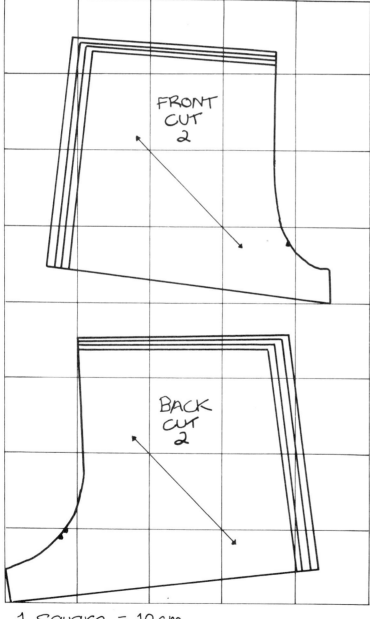

FRONT
CUT
2

BACK
CUT
2

Waist size
64 cm 25 in
67 cm 26½ in
71 cm 28 in
76 cm 30 in

1 square = 10 cm
1·5 cm seam allowance

KNICKERS

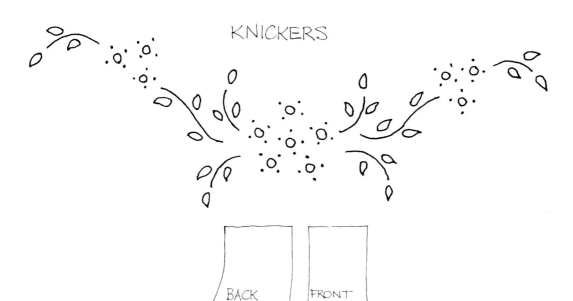

BACK   FRONT

stitch together at sides
with a narrow french seam

stitch front to back at inner
leg with a narrow french
seam

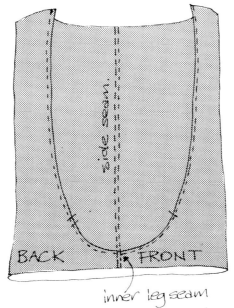

side seam.

BACK   FRONT

inner leg seam

stitch crotch seam with
very fine french seam

65

9 Bed Jacket

Sizes
Small 80–87 cm (31–34 in); Large 92–97 cm (36–38 in)

Materials

Small	Large	
90 cm (1 yd)	1 m (1 ¼ yds) x 115 cm (45 in) cotton voile, georgette, Viyella or Clydella	
5 m (5½ yds)	5.5 m (6 yds) x 5 cm (2 in) lace edging	
3 m (3½ yds)	4 m (4½ yds) x narrow lace beading (approximately 12 mm or ½ in)	
3.5 m (3¾ yds)	4 m (4½ yds) x 6 mm (¼ in) polyester satin ribbon	
1 m (1¼ yds)	1 m (1¼ yd) x 13 mm (½ in) polyester satin ribbon for tie	

Embroidery threads, one colour for the bow, two shades for the flowers, one colour for the leaves
No. 9 straw needle, no. 9 crewel needle

One of my students loved this bed jacket so much she threatened to have her tonsils out one at a time so she had two chances to wear it in hospital!

New Stitches and Techniques
Simultaneous gathering and attaching lace and beading to a raw edge by machine

Design is all worked in single strand embroidery thread

Design for left hand corner of bed jacket

Shadow Stitch

Leaves

Bullion roses

Buds

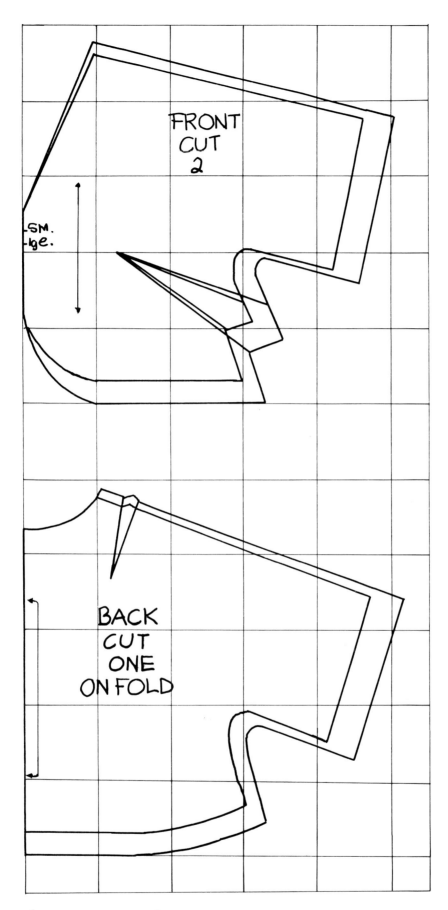

FRONT
CUT
2

SM.
lge.

BACK
CUT
ONE
ON FOLD

1 square = 10cm
1.5cm seam allowance
Small: Bust 80-87cm 31-4 in
Large: Bust 92-97cm 36-8 in

Preparation

Cut out the bed jacket and mark the darts which will *not* be sewn at this stage. Trace the large design on the right side of the jacket parallel with the front edge, keeping the tails of the design approximately 6 cm (2½ in) from raw edge. Trace the small design onto the left front, into the bottom curve about (2½ in) from raw edge.

Thread a no. 9 crewel needle with a single strand of stranded cotton and shadow stitch the bow and ribbon tails of design. Work tiny bullion roses in a single strand using two colours only, perhaps two shades of pink, and a no. 9 straw needle. Work two tiny bullions side by side in the darker shade for the centre of the rose. Six or eight twists will make a large enough bullion. Then work four or five tiny bullions in a lighter shade around the darker bullions to complete the rose. You probably won't find it necessary to end off between the roses in each little group, as the connecting threads are not really visible when the roses are so close together.

These three distances are approximately equal

The Buds

Buds are worked in the darker shade in three or four tiny satin stitches in a single thread. The calyx and sepals are worked in fly stitch, once only in a single green thread. Work a little lazy daisy leaf to each side of the stems.

Leaves

The leaves are worked in single thread lazy daisy in green in groups of threes, using a no. 9 crewel needle.

To Make Up

Once the embroidery is completed, sew the bust and shoulder darts by machine. Sew VERY FINE french seams for the shoulder and side seams. Cut the metre (1¼yds) of 13 mm (½ in) ribbon in half. Place the wrong side of the ribbon against the wrong side of the bed jacket fronts at the markings, matching the raw edges, and tack into place about 5 mm (¼ in) from the raw edge. The lace and beading are sewn over the top of the ribbon, leaving the tying ends free.

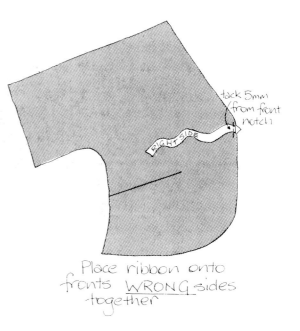

tack 5mm from front notch

RIGHT SIDE

Place ribbon onto fronts WRONG sides together

Attaching Lace by Machine

Attach the lace by machine, but if you are not a dab hand at using the sewing machine, this can be done by hand (see the note below about completing the jacket by hand).

By machine, commence at one of the side seams, place the wrong side of the lace edging against the wrong side of the bed jacket with the straight edge of lace about 5 mm (¼ in) from the raw edge of the jacket. Using the foot on the machine to hold the lace and fabric in place, lower the needle into them and, directly in front of the machine foot, make a pleat in the lace using a large pin. Hold the pleat in place with the pin and commence sewing until the needle just secures the pleat. Immediately make another pleat with the pin and continue in this manner until lace is attached all round the jacket, 5 mm (¼ in) in from the raw edges. You will find that you need more fullness in the lace round the curves of the bed jacket. The sleeves are worked in the same manner.

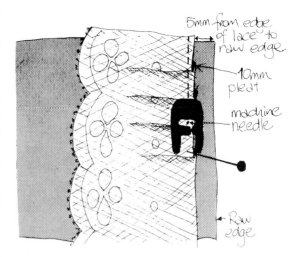

5mm from edge of lace to raw edge

10mm pleat

machine needle

Raw edge

Pleats are approximately 10mm apart

Attaching Beading by Machine

The beading is placed with the lower edge just covering the first row of machining on the lace, wrong sides together; the second edge will extend over the raw edge of the fabric at this stage. Machine the beading all round jacket on one edge only. Next, pull the scalloped edge of the lace away from the bed jacket so that the right side of the lace and the right side of jacket are now facing you, and machine the second edge of the beading into place. It will now be lying flat on the right side of the jacket. Next thread the 6 mm (¼ in) ribbon through the beading using a bodkin or small safety pin. Lap one end of the ribbon over the other and hem. Make two ribbon bows (see project 2, bullion rose and posy on washer) and stitch one on each sleeve.

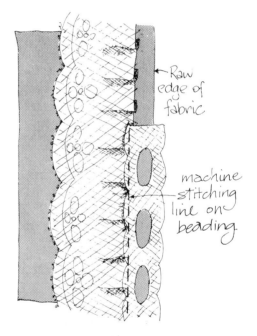

Raw edge of fabric

machine stitching line on beading.

Attaching Lace and Beading by Hand

Gather the lace first by gently drawing a thread in the straight edge of the lace until desired fullness is achieved, gather. Follow the instructions for attaching lace and beading by machine, substituting for the machine stitching a small running stitch with a back stitch every four to five stitches.

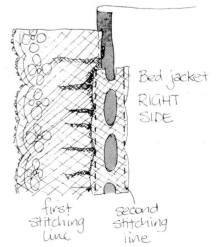

Bed jacket RIGHT SIDE

first stitching line

second stitching line

10 Coat Hanger

Materials
Wooden coat hanger (single piece of wood with metal hook – available in most supermarkets)
50 cm (¾ yd) x 115 cm (45 in) voile, linen or velveteen
1 m (1 yd) satin piping
1.5 m (1 5/8 yds) x 10 cm (4 in) medium wadding
Two pieces 12 cm (5 in) x 46 cm (18 in) thin wadding
40 cm (½ yd) x 6 mm (¼ in) polyester satin ribbon
Bias strip of matching fabric for covering hook
Stranded cotton (free choice of colours)
No. 9 crewel needle
Loop turner
Water-soluble fabric marking pen

New Stitches and Techniques
Application of piping

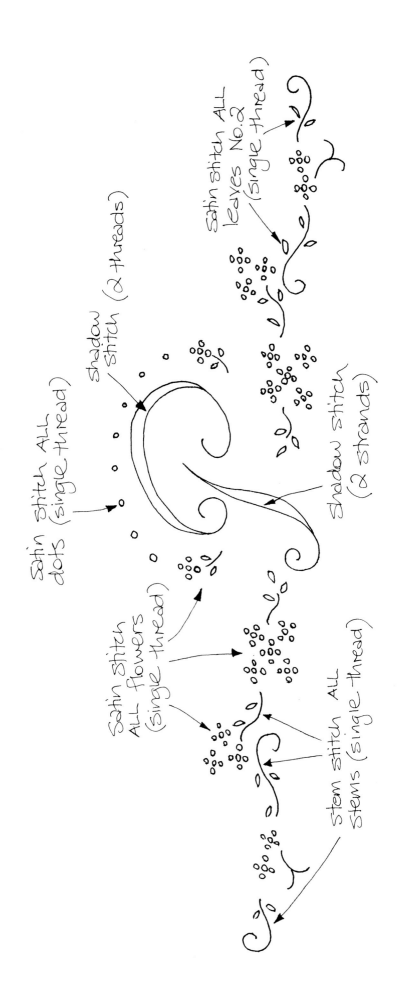

Satin stitch ALL leaves No.2 (single thread)

Shadow stitch (2 threads)

Shadow stitch (2 strands)

Satin Stitch ALL dots (single thread)

Satin stitch ALL flowers (single thread)

Stem stitch ALL stems (single thread)

BABY COAT HANGER

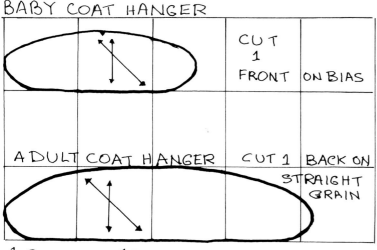

				CUT 1 FRONT	ON BIAS
ADULT COAT HANGER				CUT 1	BACK ON STRAIGHT GRAIN

1 square = 10 cm
0.5 cm seam allowance

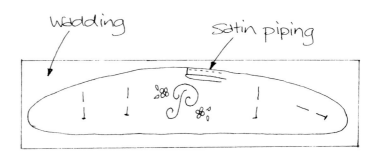

wedding

satin piping

Coat hangers make a great gift for someone special—you can never have too many. They can be made to match a blouse or nightgown, hang a wedding gown on, or be personalized with a monogram.

The front section of the covering is cut on the bias and the back section on the straight grain of the fabric.

Draw in and then embroider the design of your choice on the front section: on voile, shadow bow, flowers or monogram using single or double thread and a no. 9 crewel needle; on velveteen you could try bullion roses using three strands of stranded cotton; or on linen sew bullion roses with two strands and a no. 9 crewel needle. I usually get my students to choose their own stitches, the number of threads, designs and colours for themselves for this exercise and it is wonderful to see the variations in the final results.

Wash out the water-soluble fabric ink in cold water, dry and press the front section.

Place the front section on top of a thin piece of wadding so that the right side of the embroidery faces uppermost, and pin it into place.

Place the raw edge of satin piping against the raw edge of the fabric and wadding at the top centre front. Using a zipper foot on the sewing machine, sew as close as possible to the stitching on the satin piping. Sew the piping all round the front section, clipping the curves of the PIPING ONLY thoroughly as you go round, before sewing it into place, to achieve a nicely rounded curve. Butt the two ends of the satin piping together and trim off any excess piping. The raw ends may be turned in if you wish, but this is not absolutely necessary as they will be hidden by a ribbon bow when finished.

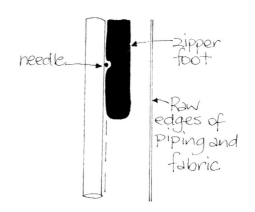

needle

zipper foot

Raw edges of piping and fabric

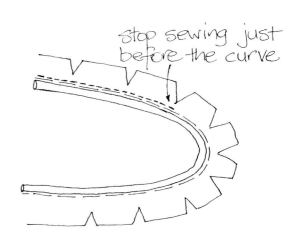

stop sewing just before the curve

Snip straight cuts into the piping stitching line. Small Vs will form

Pin the back section of the fabric to a second piece of thin wadding.

With the right sides together, pin the back and front sections of the fabric and wadding securely together, making sure that the raw edges of the fabric are all evenly matched. It may appear that the front section has stretched a little, but since it is cut on the bias, it can be easily manoeuvred into place.

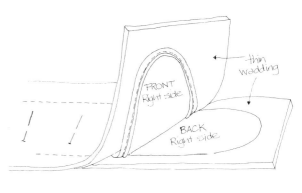

Turn the front section wadding side up so that the previous line of stitching is uppermost and begin machining, using zipper foot, along previous line of stitching, across the top only, from the middle of one end to the other, leaving a 5 mm (¼ in) gap in the stitching in the top centre front to allow for the hook. Check as you go that the edges remain evenly matched. Trim the excess wadding from the bottom edge of the coat hanger cover and a little way from top, as indicated by the dotted line on the diagram.

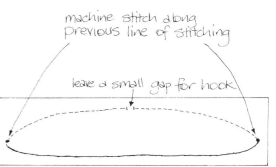

Remove all the pins and turn right sides out.

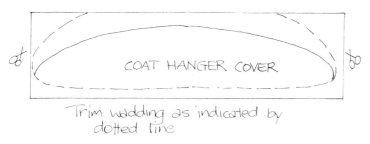

Take a strip of medium wadding and the wooden coat hanger. Holding one end of the wadding at the hanger's centre front, commence winding the wadding quite firmly around the coat hanger until the end is reached. Extend the wadding a little over the end, then commence winding it back over the first lot of winding, past the hook, and down to the other end, then back to the middle. Cut and fasten the end with a few stitches to keep the wadding from unravelling.

Slip the cover over the hook and tuck the padded coat hanger into place.

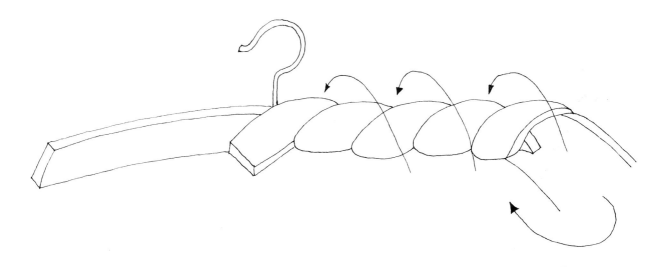

Hold the right side of the coat hanger against your body, with the cover opening uppermost. Commencing in the centre, pin the piping over the raw edges into the seam allowance of the back cover. If the pin is placed at the base of the piping, then into the seam allowance of the opposite side and the pin then pivoted backwards, it should successfully hold the opening securely closed ready for sewing. This is not the easiest operation and may take a little patience to get it straight.

Using a double thread of matching machine cotton with a small knot in the end of the thread, commence sewing at the right hand end of the hanger. Hold the hanger between the thumb and index finger of your left hand, with embroidered side of hanger farthest away from the body. Slip the needle through the stitching at the base of the piping, then take a small stitch into the seam allowance on back of the hanger, and blind stitch the edges together.

Make a rouleau to cover the metal hook on the hanger by folding in half lengthwise a bias strip of matching fabric about 17 cm (7 in) long and sew a line of machine stitching 4 mm (1/8 in) from folded edge. Trim the raw edges and turn rouleau inside out using a loop turner (the technique for making rouleau is also described in project 12, the camisole). Slip the cover over the hook, feeding the bottom edge into the coat hanger cover and securing it with a couple of firm stitches. Leave the needle and thread attached and, while you are there, secure a 40 cm (16 in) length of ribbon in the middle to the base of the hook. Tie a bow on the front of the hanger and secure it again with a stitch or two. Two lengths of contrasting ribbon of different widths make an interesting variation.

Trim the other end of the rouleau, leaving 5 mm (¼ in) of rouleau extending beyond the end of the hook. Use a single thread of matching machine cotton to secure a couple of stitches close to the raw edge. Fold the raw edge underneath the hook and wind the thread five or six times around the end of the hook and fabric to secure the rouleau firmly to the end of hook. Finish off with a couple of small satin stitches at the side.

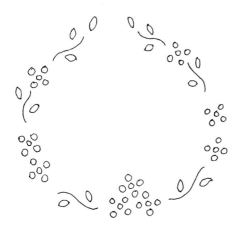

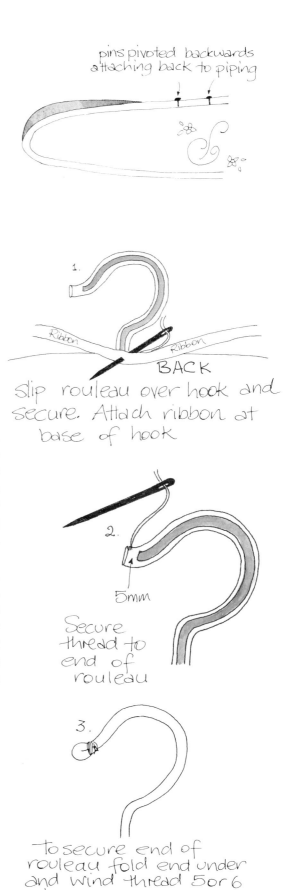

pins pivoted backwards attaching back to piping

1.

Ribbon   Ribbon

BACK

slip rouleau over hook and secure. Attach ribbon at base of hook

2.

5mm

Secure thread to end of rouleau

3.

To secure end of rouleau fold end under and wind thread 5 or 6 times around end of hook

11 Door Stop

Materials
Fade-out fabric marking pen or tailors chalk
30 cm (12 in) x 115 cm (45 in) velveteen (makes 2)
1 self-cover button, 19 mm (¾ in) diameter
1.6 m (1¾ yds) x 3 mm (1/8 in) polyester satin ribbon
30 cm (12 in) x 115 cm (45 in) calico (for insert)
Half sand/half sawdust mixture for filling
1 button to match velveteen, 15 mm (5/8 in)
Selected stranded cottons: two shades of pink, one each
of yellow and pale green
Nos 3 and 5 straw needles
Very long straight needle (about 9 cm or 3½ in long)
Strong linen mending thread
Beads can be used instead of french knots for
flower centres

The inspiration for this door stop comes from a book by Rosie Montague called Brazilian Three-Dimensional Embroidery *(Dover, New York, 1983). The stitches are fun to work and the effect is quite dramatic on velveteen.*

New Stitches and Techniques
Bullion loop rose
Pistil stitch
Bullion lazy daisy

Cut the length of velveteen in two to make two pieces measuring 30 x 57.5 cm (12 x 22½ in) each. Set one piece aside for future use. Trim the remaining piece of velveteen so it measures 27 x 53 cm (10½ x 21 in). The pieces that are trimmed off can be used to cover the button, so do not discard them. Fold the piece of velveteen in half and measure up 12.5 cm (5 in) from the fold to the centre. Mark the centre with a pin. Now measure across from edge to edge and mark the centre, moving the pin if necessary. The centre will appear to be 1 cm (3/8 in) closer to the fold but this is to allow for a 1 cm (3/8 in) seam allowance at the other end. Remove the central pin and mark this point with pencil. Using a tape measure and fade-out fabric marking pen or tailors chalk, dot a 6 cm (2½ in) circle radiating out from the central dot. On that circle now mark three equidistant spots (at 12, 4 and 8 o'clock). These are the commencement points for the roses.

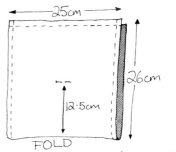

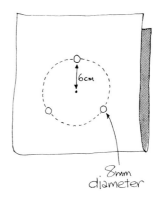

Bullion Loop Roses

Thread a no. 3 straw needle with a long length (approximately 90 cm or 1 yd) of six strands of embroidery thread. Draw a circle with the fade-out pen at one of the three points on the circle. Make this smaller circle about 8 mm (3/8 in) in diameter. This circle will become the middle of the rose. Knot the end of the embroidery cotton and bring the needle up through the velveteen from behind at some point on the small circle, point A. Put the needle in at B and bring it back out at A, pushing the shaft of the needle through almost to the eye of needle. Hold the needle between your thumb and forefinger and twist the thread clockwise round the needle, keeping the tension loose, about thirty times. Gently pull the needle through the fabric and the twists, guiding the twists round onto the velveteen to B. You should now have a bullion loop. Put the needle in at B and out at C, and pull it through. Now put the needle down at D and up at C and repeat the twists. Put the needle down at D and up again at B. Repeat these steps until a circle of bullion loops is completed, taking the final loop in behind the first loop. End off into the stitches on the back of the fabric. You should have about seven or eight loops. Work the other roses in the same manner.

Fill the centre of the flowers with about five french knots in a contrasting colour and with one twist round needle, using all six threads of cotton. Beads may be used in the centre instead of french knots.

Now measure half way between two of the roses on the circle and draw another 8 mm (3/8 in) circle. Do this twice more so that you have three small circles, one between each of the roses.

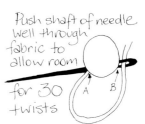

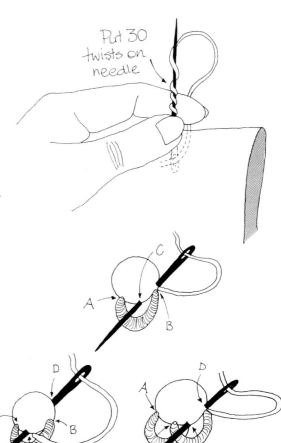

Pistil Stitch Flowers

Select a second colour of embroidery thread, and use six strands and a long thread. Thread a no. 3 straw needle and put a knot in the end of the threads. Bring needle up at a point on small circle – point A – with the fabric lying on a flat surface, such as a bread board (not a good table top in case of damage). Use your left hand and make four twists clockwise around the needle. Put the needle into the fabric at B, about 1.5 cm (5/8 in) from the edge of the small circle. Pull the needle and thread through to the back of the fabric. Bring the needle up again at C and make the next pistil stitch slightly longer than the last, fanning it out a little at the edge. Work the remainder of the circle in this fashion, with alternating long and smaller pistil stitches. End off the thread into the stitches at the back of the work. Complete the other two circles in the same manner.

Fill the centre of the flowers with french knots in six strands. Use a contrasting colour and one twist around the needle. Beads may again be used in place of the french knots.

Next place a line approximately 1 cm (3/8 in) long on a slant between each of the flowers, both roses and pistil flowers. There should be six lines in all.

Bullion Lazy Daisy

Thread a no. 5 straw needle with three strands of another colour of embroidery thread. Work four or five padding satin stitches the length of the 1 cm (3/8 in) line from A to B, bringing needle up at C. Satin stitch from the middle to the end of the padding stitches, coming to a point at the end. Return to C and satin stitch to the other end. The reason for working from the middle to the end is that it is easier to form an even shape this way. Complete all the other centres, six in all.

Choose another colour of cotton and thread a no. 5 straw needle with three strands and knot the end. Bring the needle up at D and pull the thread through. Place the needle back in at D and bring it out at E, but don't pull it through. Take the thread from point D in your right hand and twist it around the point of the needle four times in a clockwise direction, then hold the thread round the other side of the needle to form a lazy daisy back at point D before pulling the needle through. Secure the bullion by going down at F. Complete the rest of the petals on the daisy by working the four quarter points first then working two more petals between each of these. Work twelve petals in all. Work a series of french knots around the centre of the daisy in three strands of cotton with three twists to each knot.

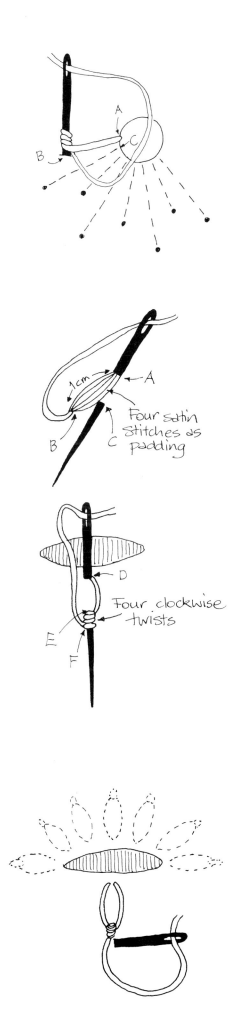

Rose Buds

Using three strands of embroidery cotton in the same colour as the bullion loop roses, thread a no. 5 straw needle and knot the end. Bring the needle up on the inside of the major circle close to the bullion loop rose at A. Put the needle back in at B, but don't pull it through, and make twenty-five twists around the needle. Pull the thread through the stitches and push the bullion into place from A to B. Put the needle back down at B and bring it up again at A. Work another bullion in the same fashion between A and C, coming back to A again. Work three pistil stitches—two short and one long—in between the two bullion stitches. Work one more bullion bud on the other side of the bullion rose, outside the major circle. Repeat this for each of the three bullion roses.

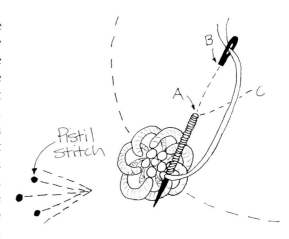

To Make Up

Turn the fabric wrong side out and, on the sewing machine, sew side seams using the 1 cm (3/8 in) seam allowance. Turn the bag right side out and set it aside.

Make a calico insert by drawing a 19.5 cm (7¾ in) diameter circle on the fabric and cut out two circles. Cut a 12 x 70 cm (5 x 28 in) strip of calico from the remaining piece. Place the raw edge of one calico circle to the raw edge of the strip and machine 1.5 cm (5/8 in) in from the edge around circle and trim the excess. Sew a seam down the strip, then join the second calico circle to other edge of the strip, leaving part of the seam open for filling. Turn the bag right side out and fill it quite full with the sand and sawdust mixture. Sew the bag closed securely. Slip the calico insert into the velveteen bag and turn in the raw edges on the velveteen for 1 cm (3/8 in) on each side and blind sew it closed with matching cotton.

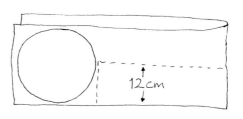

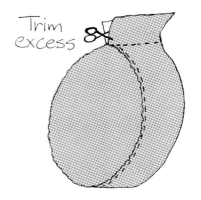

Make a covered velvet button following the directions on the packet, but first dampen the velvet being used for the button to make it easier to handle. The button is also easier to make if you use the push down method of button making. Take a 30 cm (12 in) length of linen mending thread and thread one end through the shank of the covered button. Now thread both ends of the thread through the needle and take the needle down through the centre of the door stop from front to back and out the bottom, pulling the thread right through. Turn the door stop upside down and pull the threads tight, giving the bag a shake and thump until the button is tightly in place. Thread the second, plain button onto the thread ends at the bottom and tie it in place securely with a reef knot or two.

Turn the door stop right way up. Thread the long needle with a length of linen thread, knotted at the end. Pinching the point of a corner in the fingers of your left hand, bring the needle up in the middle of the fabric, close to the insert, and twist the thread around the fabric to form a small ear at the corner. Pull the thread tight, take the needle back down through the middle of the ear to the underside, and fasten it off in stitches at the back. Treat the other three corners in the same fashion. Cut the 3 mm (1/8 in) ribbon into four pieces and tie a bow over the linen thread on all four corners.

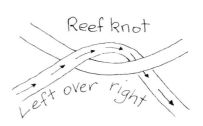

Reef knot

Left over right

Right over left

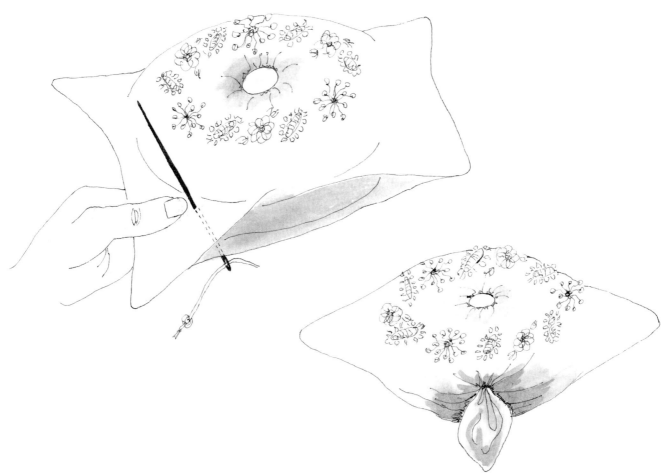

12 Camisole

Based on McCall's pattern no. 7958
Sizes
83–87 cm (32–34 in), 92–97 cm (36–38 in)

Materials

83–87 cm	92–97 cm
80 cm (7/8 yd)	90 cm (1 yd) x 115 cm (45 in) voile, cotton or batiste
1 m (1¼ yds)	1.1 m (1¼ yds) x 13 mm (½ in) lace edging
60 cm (¾ yd)	70 cm (7/8 yd) x 13 mm (½ in) insertion lace (with straight edges)

Stranded cotton to match (one colour only)
No. 9 crewel needle
Loop turner

Once you have mastered the basic techniques outlined in this chapter you can experiment with bigger and more elaborate designs and more complex treatment of the stitches, such as padding. Here, however, I have tried to keep the design and technique fairly basic. It is quite repetitive work but the rewards are worth it.

Cut out the camisole as directed on the pattern. Find the centre of the yoke front by folding it in four, and mark it with a pin. Centre the design under the pin and trace onto fabric using a water-soluble fabric marking pen.

New Stitches and Techniques
Broderie anglaise
Rouleau
Lace insertion
Shell hemming

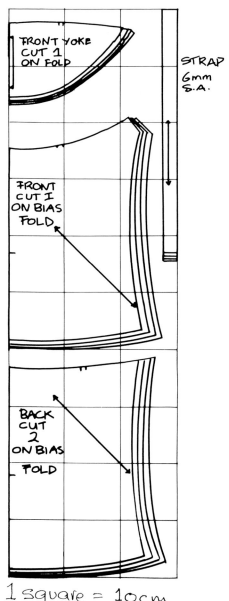

1 square = 10cm
1·5cm seam allowance
Bust size 83cm 32½ in
87cm 34 in
92cm 36 in
97cm 38 in

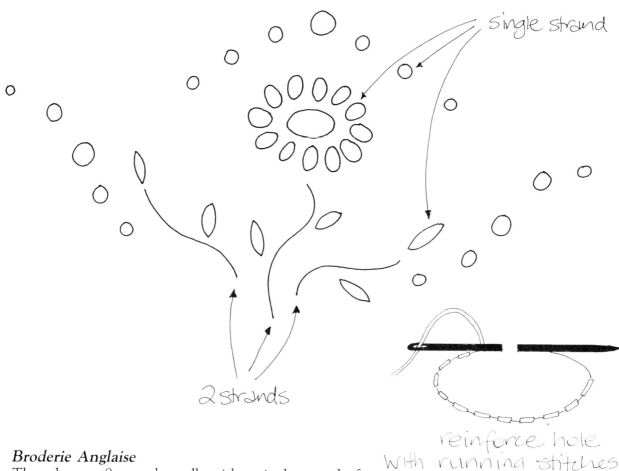

single strand

2 strands

Broderie Anglaise

Thread a no. 9 crewel needle with a single strand of embroidery thread. As this camisole is an undergarment, it is advisable to use a matching or light coloured embroidery cotton. Commence by working a small running stitch around the outline of the daisy centre. Then snip the fabric in the centre of the stitching, both lengthwise and crosswise, using sharp, pointed scissors. Hold the daisy centre firmly over the index finger of your left hand, and use the point of a needle to tuck the raw edges under, between the fabric and your finger, sliding the needle from top to bottom down the outline. Getting all the raw edges tucked under neatly is probably the hardest part of the work. Then commence overcasting stitch around the outline, over the running stitch, keeping the raw edges tucked under at all times. Try to keep an even tension. If the overcasting is pulled tight it may separate the stitches from the fabric, which is undesirable. Any excess raw edge may be trimmed away later from the back of the work. To end off, take the thread to the back of the work and darn it back through the completed stitches for about 3–4 mm (1/8 in). Work the rest of petals and leaves in the same manner, taking particular care with the small petals of the daisy.

The large eyelets are worked in the same manner, by snipping the fabric in the centre of the stitching. The small eyelets are worked by using a stiletto to punch the hole. Work a running stitch around the hole and pierce with the stiletto before overcasting. Stems are worked in two strands of the same colour embroidery cotton in stem stitch.

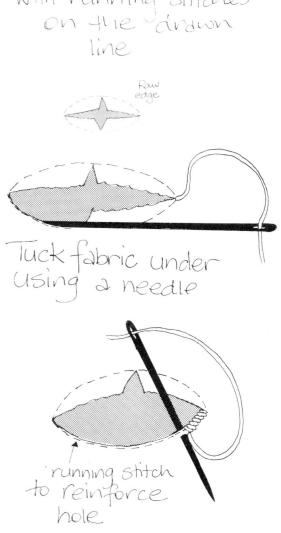

reinforce hole
with running stitches
on the drawn
line

Raw
edge

Tuck fabric under
using a needle

running stitch
to reinforce
hole

84

To Make Up

Machine stitch the front 1.5 cm (5/8 in) in from the raw edge along the seam allowance line around the curve. Trim the seam allowance away, leaving the machine stitching on the very edge of the fabric on both the yoke and front round curves. With RIGHT sides together, pin the insertion lace around the lower curved edge of yoke. Hold the work with the WRONG SIDE OF YOKE towards you. Roll and whip the edge of the yoke, attaching the insertion lace at the same time. Remove the pins one at a time as you come to them. The pins are to help prevent stretching of either the lace or fabric. The line of machine stitching is to prevent the fabric stretching out of shape, as it is cut on the bias. Press.

Next find the centre front of the yoke and camisole front and mark with a pin in each. With RIGHT sides together pin the yoke insertion to the camisole front, matching centre fronts. Continue pinning the insertion to the front round curve, stretching or easing until the yoke fits the front. With the WRONG side of the front towards you, roll and whip the edge of the front, attaching the insertion lace at the same time, thus joining the yoke to the front.

Join the front to the back at the sides with french seams. Machine stitch around the top of the camisole front and back about 1 cm (3/8 in) in from the raw edge. Trim away the fabric, leaving the machine stitching on the edge. With RIGHT sides together, pin the edging lace around the top of the camisole, beginning and ending at a side seam. With the WRONG side of the garment facing you, roll and whip the top edge, joining the edging lace at the same time and removing the pins one at a time as you go. Join the ends of the lace.

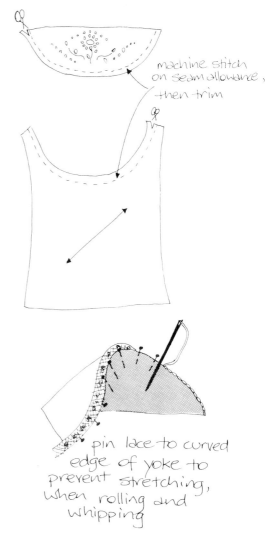

machine stitch on seam allowance, then trim

pin lace to curved edge of yoke to prevent stretching, when rolling and whipping

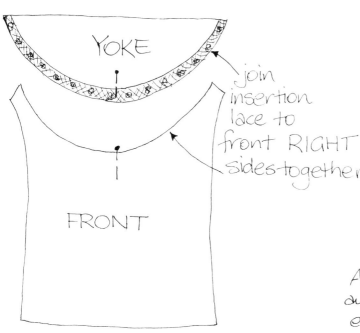

YOKE

FRONT

join insertion lace to front RIGHT sides together

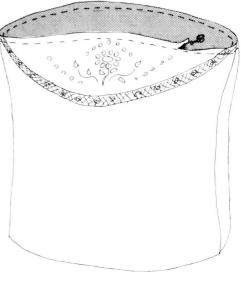

After trimming seam allowance away, whip and roll lace edging to top of camisole RIGHT sides together

Shoulder Straps

Fold the shoulder strap piece in half lengthwise, RIGHT sides together. Stitch the long edges together along the seam allowance line. Turn right side out with a loop turner. Turn up the end of strap and pin it on the back in the position marked on the pattern, level with the bottom edge of lace. Place the seams of the straps towards the arms. Try on the camisole, adjusting the straps; pin them into position and sew. Stitch the straps in position across the bottom and up the sides to the top of the lace, across the lace and back down to the bottom so the straps are quite secure.

machine stitch on seam line then trim to 5mm

Use loop turner to turn rouleau

Turn rouleau RIGHT side out

Tuck in tail when stitching rouleau in place

Shell Hemming

Fold and tack a narrow double hem, about 5 mm (¼ in) wide, along the bottom of the camisole. Using machine cotton and a no. 9 crewel needle, attach the thread with a knot hidden inside the hem. Work three or four small running stitches through the bottom of the hem, through all thicknesses. Take the needle and thread right over and around the hem, completely encasing the hem in thread and emerging just below the last running stitch. Repeat this stitch once more and pull the thread taut. Continue with the running stitches and the encasing stitch right around the hem. A blind hem stitch may be used instead of a running stitch. Shell hemming makes a very pretty edging for lingerie. It can also be used as a decorative stitch on a pin tuck.

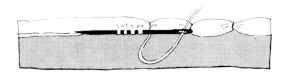

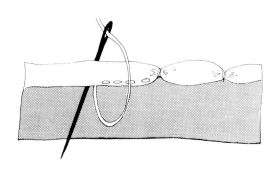

13 Continental Pillow
No. 1

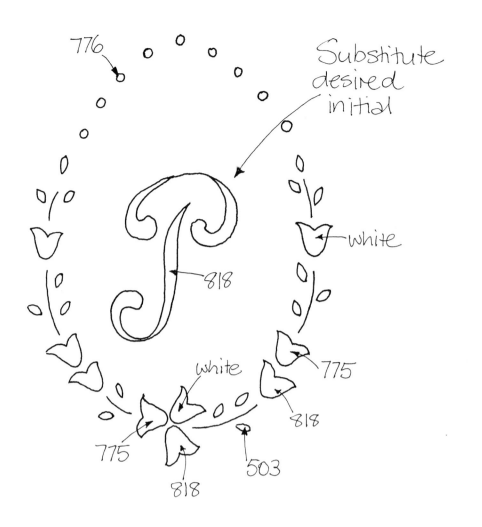

776

Substitute
desired
initial

818

white

white

775

818

775

503

818

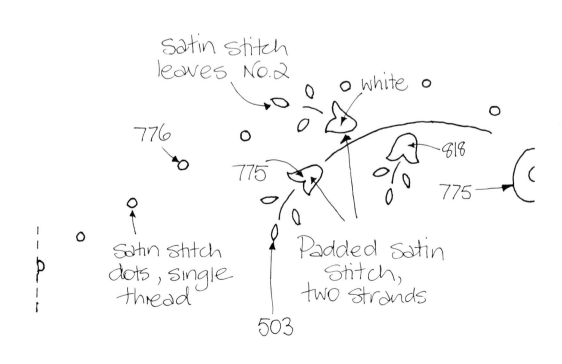

Satin stitch
leaves No.2

white

818

775

776

775

Satin stitch
dots, single
thread

503

Padded satin
stitch,
two strands

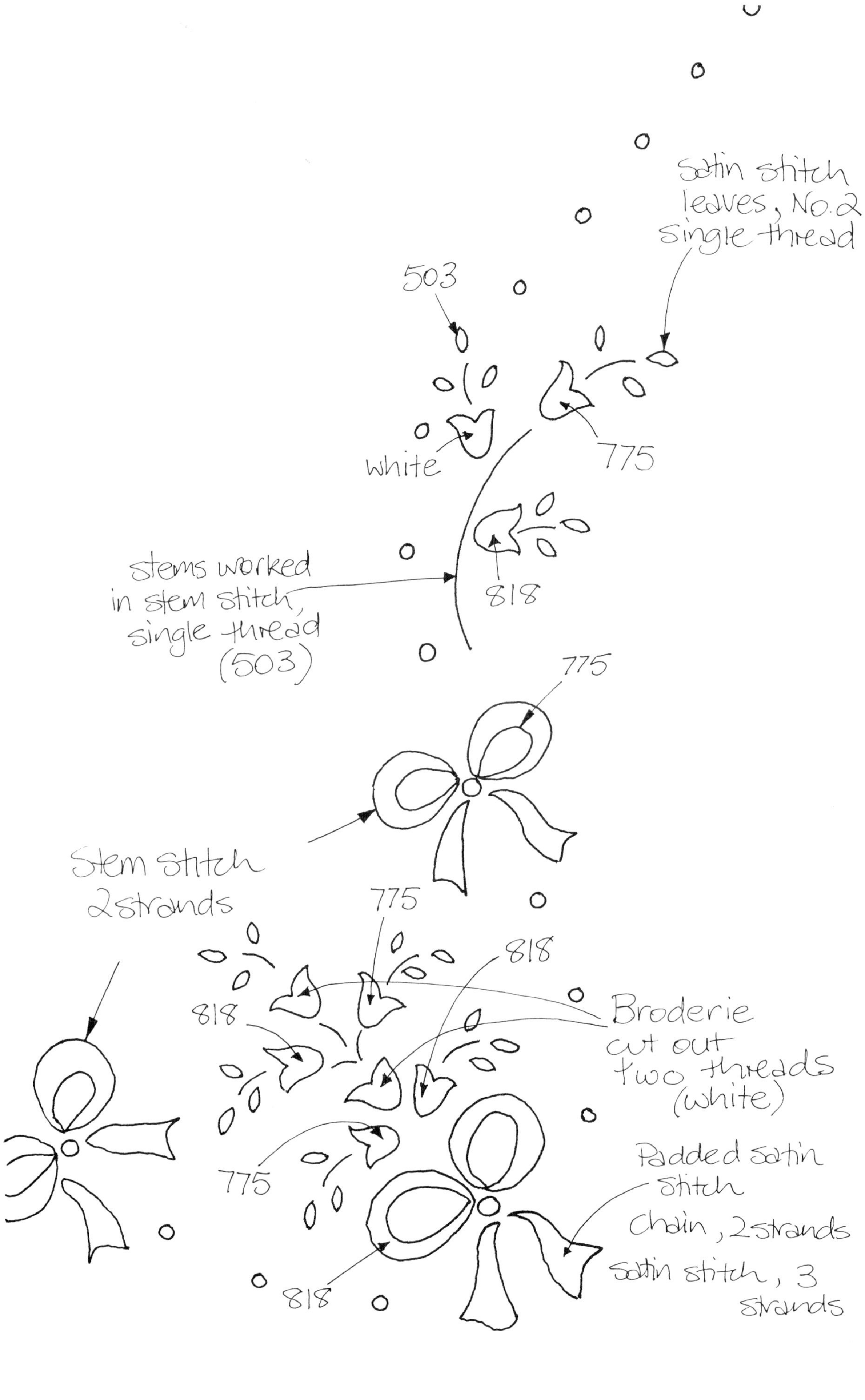

Satin stitch
leaves, No.2
single thread

503

white

775

stems worked
in stem stitch,
single thread
(503)

818

775

Stem stitch
2 strands

775

818

818

775

Broderie
cut out
two threads
(white)

Padded satin
stitch

Chain, 2 strands

Satin stitch, 3
strands

818

89

Materials

65 cm (26 in) x 65 cm (26 in) pillow

1.6 m (1¾ yds) x 90 cm (36 in) handkerchief linen or cotton

3 m (3 3/8 yds) x 7 cm (2 3/4 in) broderie anglaise or lace

2.5 m (2¾ yds) broderie anglaise beading or lace beading (any width)

4 m (4½ yds) ribbon to fit through beading

4 buttons 13 mm (½ in) diameter

Dressmakers carbon paper

Water-soluble fabric marking pen

Stranded cottons. Suggested colours: DMC white, 775, 818, 776, 503

No. 9 crewel needle

Continental or European pillows are large and square. The sizes may vary considerably, but the requirements above are for a 65 x 65 cm (26 x 26 in) size. If your pillow is larger you will need to adjust your material requirements accordingly. The fabric should be pre-shrunk by washing first, as linen particularly tends to shrink a little.

Front

Cut a 68 x 68 cm (27 x 27 in) square of fabric and fold it into quarters to find the middle point. Mark this point with a pin or dot. Use a tape measure to measure from the centre point to each corner in turn and make a dot at 32 cm (12½ in) from the centre. This will be the centre of the satin stitch bow and will be the key point to lining up the design. The design may be transferred by using dressmakers carbon or a water-soluble marking pen. Place the design on one corner of the fabric, centring the satin stitch bow over the dot and lining up the design so that the dots are equidistant from the raw edges of the fabric. Pin the design in place and trace it using your chosen method. Trace the central design too, substituting your own monogram for the P used here. The design is placed in all four corners so that the dots make a continuous wavy line.

New Stitches and Techniques

Chain stitch

Padded satin stitch

Attaching lace by machine

Mitred corners

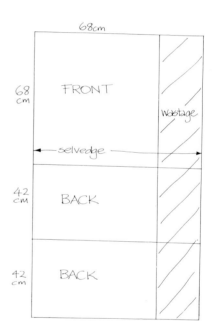

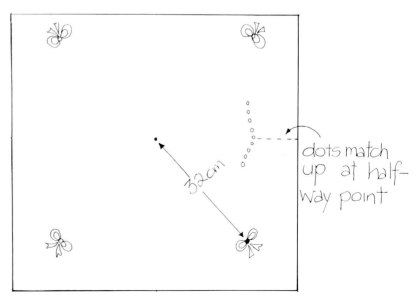

Padded Satin Stitch Bow

Thread a no. 9 crewel needle with two strands of embroidery cotton in selected colour. Commence work with a few small running stitches towards the centre of the bow, along one of the tails. Now turn your work and chain stitch back over the running stitches, filling the area between the lines with chain stitch.

Chain Stitch

The needle goes in at A and comes out at B, with the thread around the needle as in lazy daisy stitch. Pull the thread through but, instead of anchoring the stitch, the needle goes back into the fabric just inside the loop at B so that the next chain commences inside the previous chain. Fill the entire bow with chain stitch to act as a padding for the satin stitch.

Satin Stitch

Now thread the needle with three strands of embroidery thread. Commence with three running stitches towards the centre and work back with satin stitch. To achieve a smooth finish to satin stitch, use the thread to guide your next stitch until you achieve the desired effect. In other words, lay the thread for the next stitch in place and then put needle down into fabric. Allow room for the thickness of the thread too, so that stitches are not packed on top of each other. Each thread should lie directly beside the last one. When rounding the loops of the bow, adjust the stitches slightly, packing them up more closely on the inside of loop and spreading them out a little on the outside of the loop. When working the tails of the bow, satin stitch to the point at which the tail divides. Work one side of the tail, then bring the needle back underneath to the dividing point and work the other side of the tail. Finish off by darning into the back of the threads. The other two bows on each corner of the design are worked in two strands of cotton in stem stitch. The centres of these two bows are worked in satin stitch in the same colour as the dots in satin stitch.

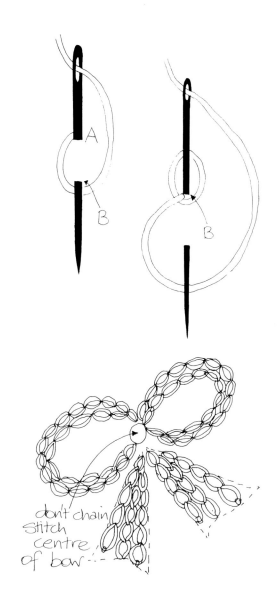

don't chain stitch centre of bow ·--

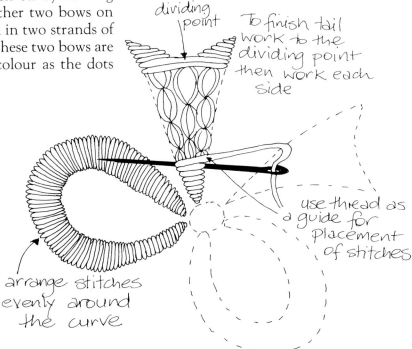

dividing point

To finish tail work to the dividing point then work each side

use thread as a guide for placement of stitches

arrange stitches evenly around the curve

Flowers

The satin stitch flowers are worked in the same method as the satin stitch bow. The flowers are first padded with two strands of embroidery cotton in chain stitch. Work satin stitch over the top in two strands of embroidery cotton in the same colour. Work from the base of the flower towards two points, working first one point then the other, following the outline of the transfer.

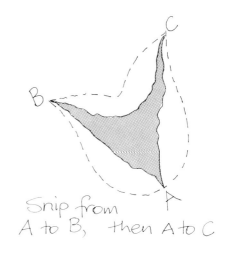

Snip from A to B, then A to C

The broderie anglaise flowers are worked in two strands of embroidery cotton. Commencing at the base of the flower, work a small running stitch around the outline. When this is completed, use a sharp, pointed pair of scissors to snip the centre of the flower from A to B and A to C, then trim a little more from the flap in the centre. Holding the work firmly over the index finger of your left hand, tuck the raw edges under, using the point of a needle so that the line of small running stitches is now on the inside edge of the flower. Satin stitch over the running stitches, keeping an even tension. If these stitches are pulled too tightly, the work will pull away from the rest of the fabric, so take your time and work gently. It is useful to guide the threads into place with the thumb of your left hand (see the camisole).

HOLE

Finished broderie anglaise flower

The stems are worked in a single strand of embroidery cotton in stem stitch. Dots are worked in a single strand of embroidery cotton in satin stitch, with about fifteen to sixteen stitches to each dot. Leaves are worked in single thread satin stitch using method no. 2 (see collars).

Monogram

Your monogram in the centre of the pillow is worked in two strands of embroidery cotton for chain stitch padding and two strands for satin stitch over the top of the chain stitch.

Wash out the transfer markings in cold water.

Making Up the Back

From the remaining piece of material cut two pieces measuring 40 x 68 cm (16 x 27 in) for the back. Fold and press 1 cm (3/8 in) in on one long edge of the two back pieces of fabric. Fold again and press a 2.5 cm (1 in) hem. This hem may be blind hemmed by hand or machine stitched. Place one hem on top of the other, RIGHT side to WRONG side, and pin in place. Now mark four buttonholes across the hem at intervals of 13 cm (5 in), which leaves extra space at the sides to include a seam allowance (the seams will be sewn 1.5 cm or 5/8 in wide). Make the buttonholes either by hand or by machine to fit buttons. Sew on buttons.

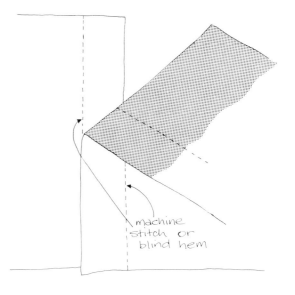

machine stitch or blind hem

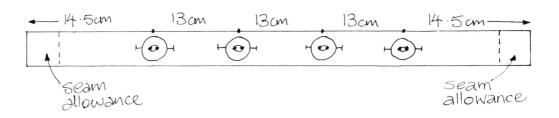

14·5cm   13cm   13cm   13cm   14·5cm

seam allowance   seam allowance

92

To Attach Lace

Lie the finished panel out on a flat surface RIGHT side up. Place the edging broderie on the pillow case front with the edge of lace level with the raw edge of the fabric. Pin the lace until the first corner is reached. Put the point of a pin into the lace in the very outer corner and hold it while at the same time folding the lace back on itself. Now peel back the outer edge of the lace to run down the next side of the pillow case, forming a mitred corner. Pin in place. Continue in this manner until the last corner is reached. Place the point of a pin in the inner corner of the lace at the point where it joins the existing lace. Fold the lace under and at right angles to form a mitred corner. Pin in place. Detach the mitred corners of the broderie at a 45 degree angle from the fabric and sew along the fold from behind. Sew the seam twice on the same line. Trim away the excess broderie and finish the raw edges by overlocking on the machine or rolling and whipping by hand.

Now machine the inner raw edge of the broderie to the pillow case along all four sides. Finish the raw edge of the broderie by placing a round of eyelet or beading broderie over the top, mitring the corners as you did on the broderie. Don't cut away the corners of the beading. The beading is best machine stitched in place. You may need to trim the raw edges of the broderie beading first or fold the raw edges under before sewing it in place over the bottom edge of the broderie edging. Some beading comes without raw edges.

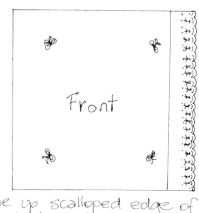

Line up scalloped edge of broderie with raw edge of fabric

TO MITRE A CORNER

Hold broderie in place with pin

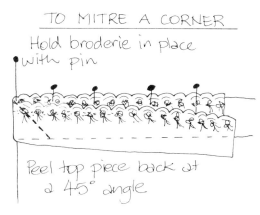

Peel top piece back at a 45° angle

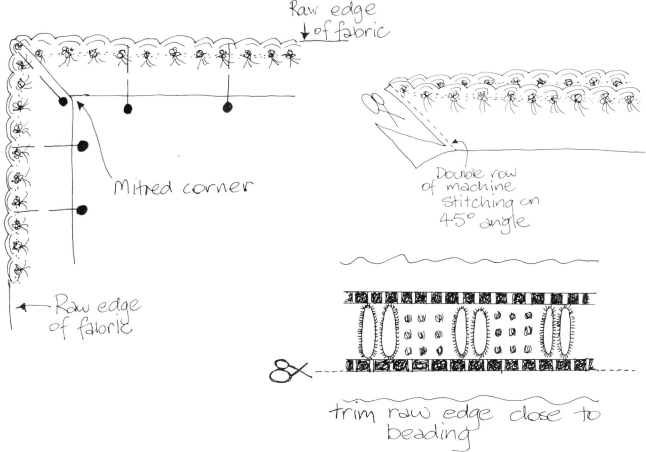

Raw edge of fabric

Mitred corner

Raw edge of fabric

Double row of machine stitching on 45° angle

trim raw edge close to beading

To Complete the Pillow

Now place the front and back pillow case pieces WRONG sides together. Make sure the buttons are fastened on the back section. Run a 1 cm (3/8 in) seam around the four sides of the pillow case taking care not to catch in broderie. Trim the raw edges back leaving a 4 mm (¼ in) seam. Turn the pillow case wrong side out by opening the buttons at the back. Complete 5 mm (¼ in) french seam, again taking care not to catch the lace into the seam. Turn the pillow case right side out. Cut the ribbon into four pieces, thread the ribbons through the beading and tie bows in the corners. Catch the bows with a stitch from behind so they don't come undone in the wash.

Put the pillow into the pillow case and stand back to admire your work.

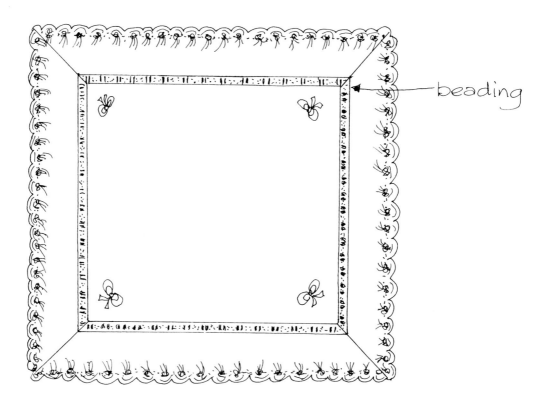

beading

14 Continental Pillow
No. 2

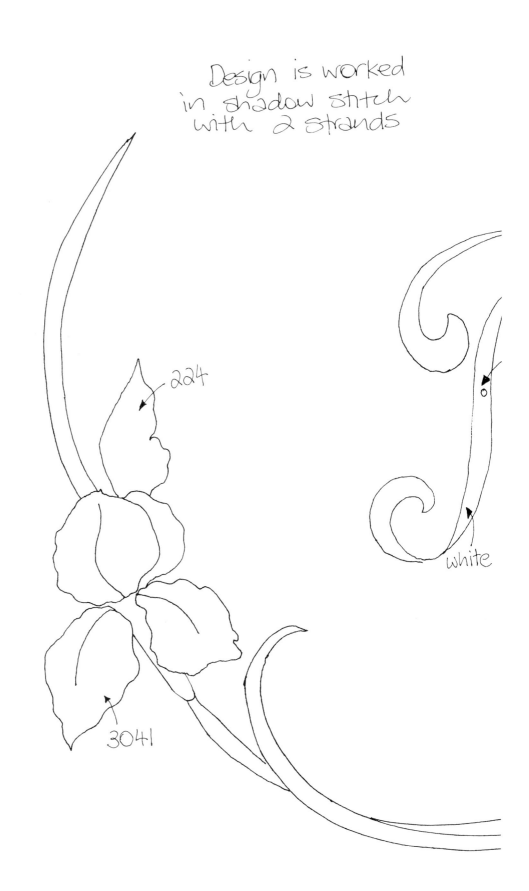

Design is worked
in shadow stitch
with 2 strands

224

white

3041

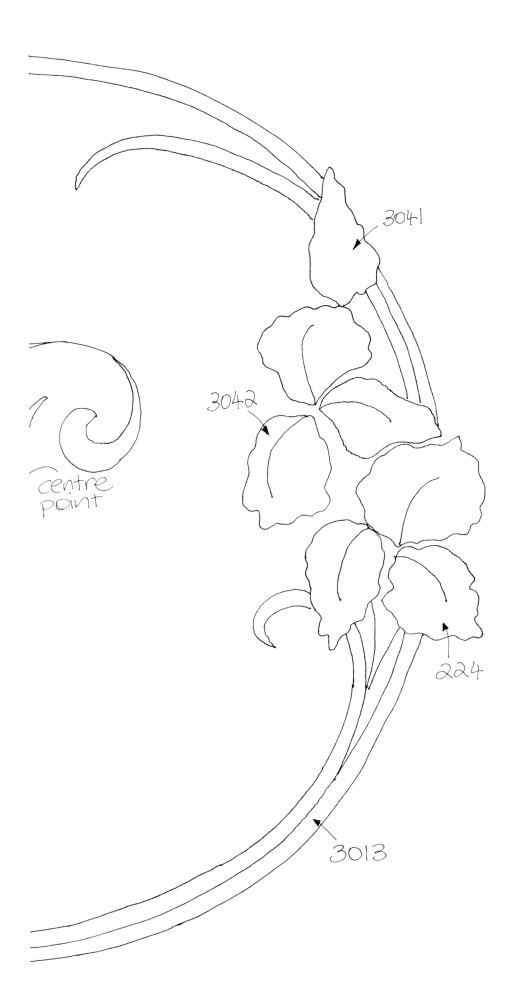

3041

3042

224

centre
point

3013

97

Materials

65 cm (26 in) x 65 cm (26 in) pillow
1.15 m (45 in) x 115 cm (45 in) voile
3.1 m (3½ yds) x 7 cm (2¾ in) lace edging
2.5 m (2¾ yds) lace beading (any width)
4 m (4½ yds) ribbon to fit through beading
4 buttons 10 mm (3/8 in) diameter
Stranded cotton. Suggested colours: DMC white, 224,
3013, 3041, 3042
Machine cotton
Water-soluble fabric marking pen
No. 9 crewel needle
Optional satin underslip: 1.5 m (1¾ yds) x 115 (45 in)

*The iris or fleur de Louis, believed to have been named after
the French kings who chose the iris for their emblem, is one
of my favourite flowers. It was my school emblem too and
many wonderful varieties are grown in the gardens of
Frensham at Mittagong. So I like to reproduce these beautiful
flowers in my embroidery, though it is impossible to do justice
to the wonderful colours with which nature has endowed the
iris. If you have practised the shadow stitch in one of the
previous projects (such as the shoe bag), you should find this
pillow slip relatively quick and easy.*

Pull a thread to ensure that the fabric is straight before
cutting. Cut the voile as indicated by the dotted line
on diagram. Fold the front piece in four and mark the
centre with a pin. Place the voile right side up over the
design, matching the two centre points, and trace with
a water-soluble fabric marking pen.

Shadow Stitch

Thread a no. 9 crewel needle with two strands of
embroidery cotton for the iris. The threads will need
to be quite long—about 1 m (1 yd)—to avoid continual
ending off. Commence the shadow stitch on the
WRONG side of the work. As there is a considerable
distance to span, take care not to pull the threads too
tightly or the fabric will pucker. You may prefer to use
an embroidery hoop, but I work with the design held
over the index finger of my left hand. Take the stitches
from the sides of the petals to the centre line as far as
the centre line extends, then span the entire distance
to the other side of the petal until the tip is reached.
Once the tip is reached and all stitches on the front of
work are lined up, turn the work. Darn a thread down
the edge of the petal, through the stitches only, and
commence shadow stitching again. Work back towards
the beginning of the petal, this time picking up only the
stitches down the centre line of petal. This way there
will only be one line of small backstitches down middle
of the iris petal on the right side of the work and the
whole petal will be shadow stitched.

Work all the petals in this manner. Where there is
a common line in the design between two petals, pick
up the stitches only when shadow stitching the line the
second time. Work all the flowers first then the stalks
and leaves using the same method.

New Stitches and Techniques
Pin tucks

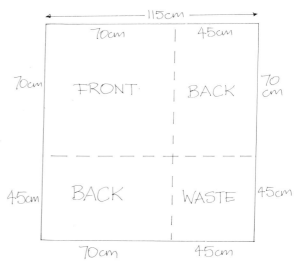

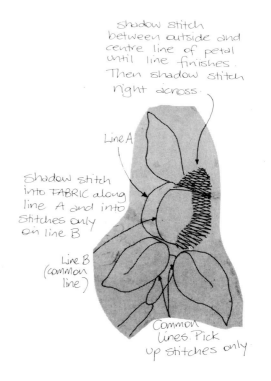

shadow stitch
between outside and
centre line of petal
until line finishes.
Then shadow stitch
right across.

Line A

Shadow stitch
into FABRIC along
line A and into
stitches only
on line B

Line B
(common
line)

Common
lines. Pick
up stitches only

98

The monogram is also shadow stitched from the back of the work. Where the line becomes single, work in stem stitch on the back of the work, taking each stitch back to the same hole where the previous stitch ended.

Once the embroidery is completed, wash out the water-soluble pen markings and press. Wash the two back panels at the same time in case there is any shrinkage.

Pin Tucks

Measure 17 cm (6½ in) from the centre point of the front out towards each side edge and mark with a pin. Draw a single thread from edge to edge along the line marked by the pin to form a square around the design. This will be your guide for making the first pin tucks. Fold the fabric on one of the side edges along the drawn thread line and either work the pin tuck by hand with small running stitches or by machine, making the pin tuck approximately a needle width wide. Draw the next thread for pin tuck about 12 mm (½ in) outside the first one and work a pin tuck in same manner. Work a third pin tuck to correspond with the first two. Press the tucks towards the outside edge then make three more tucks on each of the other three sides of the front in the same manner, pressing all the pin tucks towards the outer edges.

Square off the front pillow slip now to measure 68 x 68 cm (27 x 27 in), and make up following the directions in continental pillow no. 1.

The appearance of the pillow will be greatly enhanced if a satin underslip is used. Follow the instructions for making up the voile pillow slip, omitting embroidery and pin tucks.

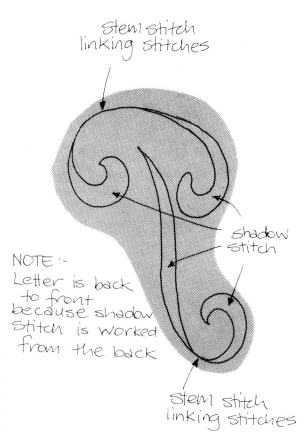

Stem stitch
linking stitches

shadow
stitch

NOTE :-
Letter is back
to front
because shadow
stitch is worked
from the back

Stem stitch
linking stitches

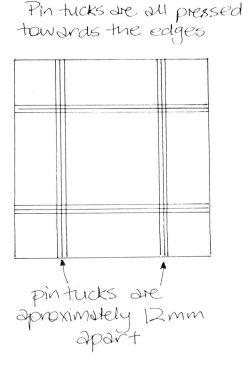

Pin tucks are all pressed
towards the edges

pin tucks are
aproximately 12mm
apart

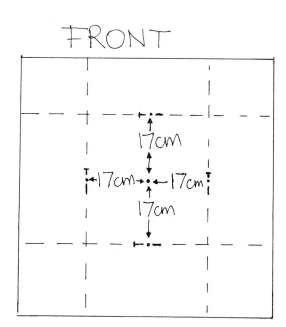

FRONT

17cm

17cm → ← 17cm

17cm

Draw one thread only
along lines marked
by pins

15 Bridge Cloth

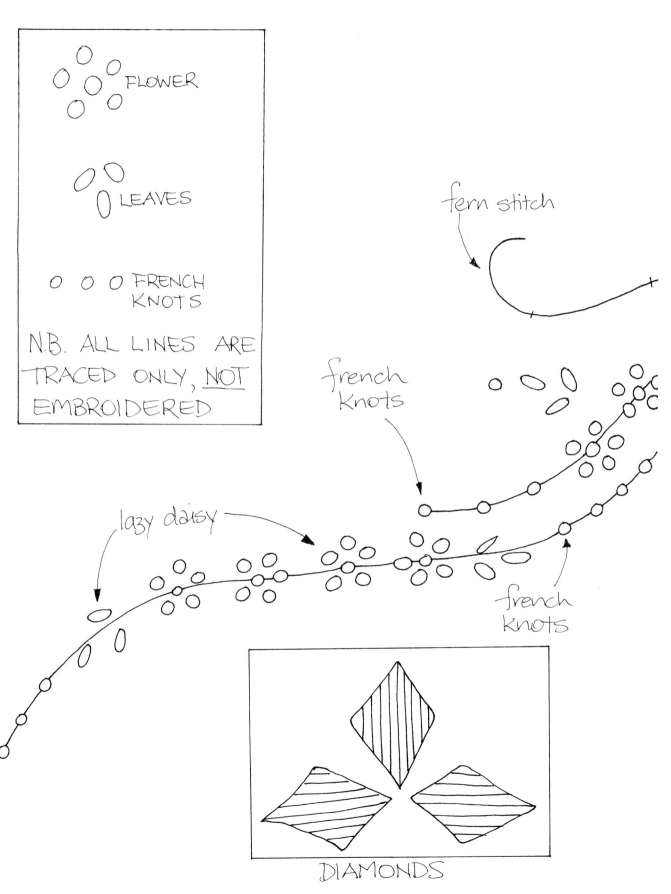

FLOWER

LEAVES

FRENCH KNOTS

N.B. ALL LINES ARE TRACED ONLY, NOT EMBROIDERED

fern stitch

french knots

lazy daisy

french knots

DIAMONDS

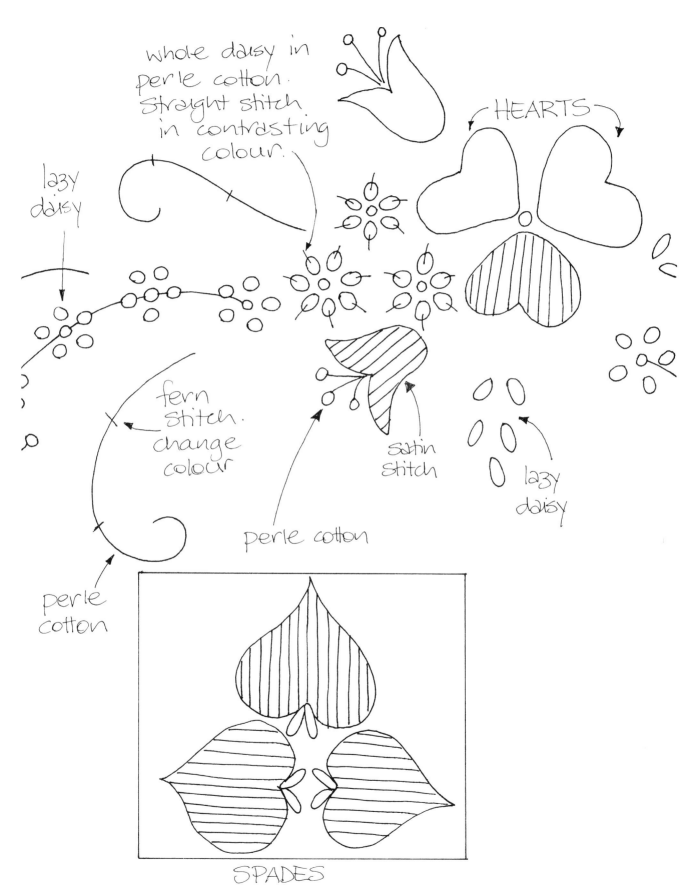

whole daisy in
perle cotton.
Straight stitch
in contrasting
colour.

HEARTS

lazy
daisy

fern
stitch.
change
colour

satin
stitch

lazy
daisy

perle
cotton

perle cotton

SPADES

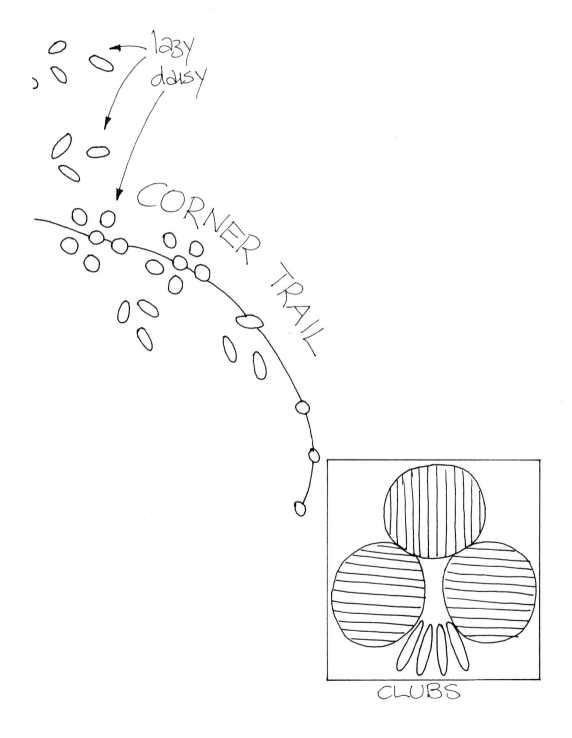

lazy
daisy

CORNER TRAIL

CLUBS

Materials

1.15 cm (1¼ yds) x 115 cm (45 in) velveteen (suggest dark green)

5 m (5½ yds) x 1.5 cm (5/8 in) grosgrain ribbon

Tapestry wools. Suggested DMC colours:
  2 skeins dark colour (7194)
  2 skeins medium colour (7121)
  1 skein green (7925)
  2 skeins contrast colour (7905, 7191)

Perle cotton, DMC no. 3 in two shades of one colour (754 and 758)

1 pkt 18/24 chenille needles

Tracing paper

Dressmakers carbon paper

Tracing wheel

Fade-out marker pen or tailors chalk

This bridge cloth has been designed with a view to leaving the maximum amount of unencumbered space for serious bridge players and a maximum amount of embroidery to satisfy the urge of the needleworker. The two should be compatible, as the design drifts on and off the bridge table. I have also, contrary to advice, included in each corner each of the four suits slightly disguised. If this offends the potential needleworker, I suggest you choose the design you like best and work the same one in all four corners.

First trace the design onto the transparent tracing paper. To place the design correctly on the fabric, fold it into four, measure 46 cm (18 in) on a diagonal line from the folded corner. Mark with a pin. Mark each corner in the same manner. Trace and work only one corner at a time, as the design wears off and fades as you work.

To transfer the design onto velveteen, place dressmakers carbon paper, carbon side down, onto the right side of the velveteen and centre the design over the top, placing the middle of the spades, hearts, diamonds or clubs over the pin and swinging the design until the corner trail points to the corner of the velveteen. With a tracing wheel, mark the long trails and other markings. Daisies may be marked with an X only instead of tracing out the individual petals. Similarly, there is no need to mark the feathery trails, just a line will do. The same applies to trails of leaves and centre of flowers etc. These can be worked in later using the design as a guide.

The design covers only half of the corner. The other half of the corner is a mirror image of the first half, so lift the design tracing and turn it over before tracing the second half. There is no need to retrace parts of design common to both halves, even though they may not line up exactly. Once the design is marked out in carbon, it is then advisable to go over this again with tailors chalk or fade-out pen to ensure the design remains visible for the duration of embroidery.

New Stitches and Techniques

Satin stitch in wool

Fern stitch

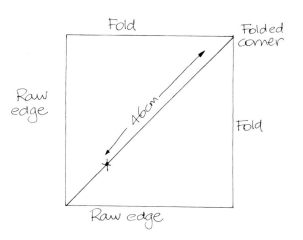

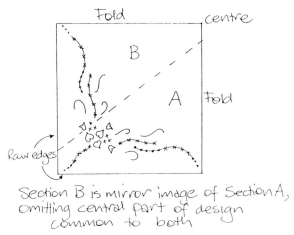

Section B is mirror image of Section A, omitting central part of design common to both

Satin Stitch

Thread a no. 18 chenille needle with a length of selected colour tapestry wool and commence satin stitch on the card suits. Work from the middle to either side, because it is then easier to get the design even. Commence with a running stitch through the centre, then pad the area with satin stitches. Always leave room for the thickness of the thread so that each thread lies directly beside the last one and they do not overlap. It is helpful to use the thread as a guide, placing it where it will ultimately lie before taking a stitch, always keeping the thread to the right of the needle. Once you have completed half of the design, turn your work upside down and complete the other half of the design. To end off, take the wool to the back of the work and darn the thread back and forth into the stitches on the back. If you darn through the thread you are using a few times, it helps to secure the thread further.

Fern Stitch

To work fern stitch, commence at the base of the line with the dark coloured thread and make short straight stitches up the line, working first one side and then the other. There is no stitch down the middle of the line – the stitches on either side create an illusion of a central stalk. Change the thread to the pale shade a third of the way up and for the last third use perle cotton.

Daisies

Daisies are worked in lazy daisy stitch and the centres in french knots. Daisies close to the central design with more than five petals are worked in perle cotton. Using two shades of perle cotton, commence the daisy in the dark shade and work five or six lazy daisy stitches in a circle. It is helpful to draw a small circle for the middle first and then work around this. Using a lighter shade, work around the daisy placing a straight stitch up through the centre of each petal at A and down outside the petal at B. French knots are worked in the centre of each daisy and at the end of trails, using one twist only around the needle.

Stamens in the bell flowers are worked in perle cotton in pistil stitch.

Leaves are worked in lazy daisy stitch in groups of five and three as shown on the design.

To Make Up

Bind the edge of the bridge cloth with grosgrain ribbon. Press a 1 cm (3/8 in) hem towards the right side of the fabric all around the cloth. Place the grosgrain ribbon over the hem, taking the ribbon right to the folded edge and stitching by machine along both edges of the ribbon in matching thread. Mitre the corners of the ribbon (see the continental pillow no. 1).

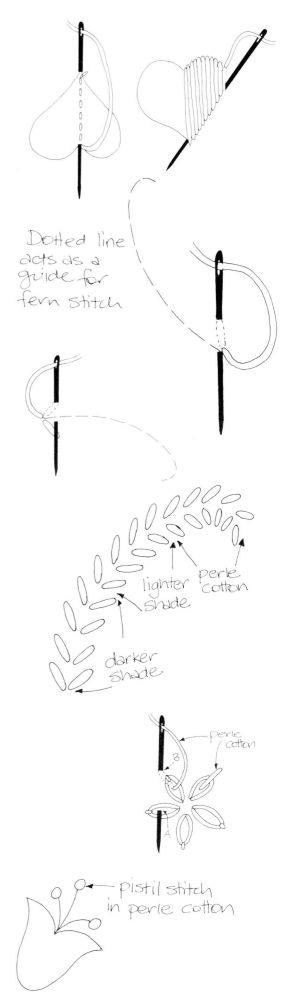

Dotted line acts as a guide for fern stitch

lighter shade

perle cotton

darker shade

perle cotton

B

A

pistil stitch in perle cotton

16 Sloppy Joe with Ribbon Roses

Materials

1 sloppy joe or sweatshirt (polycotton)
50 cm (20 in) x 22 mm (7/8 in) polyester satin ribbon for each rose.
4 cm (1½ in) x 22 mm (7/8 in) polyester satin ribbon for bud
12 cm (5 in) x 7 cm (2¾ in) material for stalk with matching cotton thread
7 cm (2¾ in) x 7 cm (2¾ in) material for pot with matching thread
Stranded cottons: green and colour to contrast with pot material
2 m (2¼ yds) x 3 mm (1/8 in) polyester satin ribbon
Satay stick
Nos. 4–5 straw needle, no. 9 crewel needle
Water-soluble fabric marking pen

This washes like a dream in the washing machine if the sloppy joe and ribbon contain polyester. And there is no need to iron.

Ribbon Roses

Thread a no. 4 or 5 straw needle with a double length of machine cotton knotted at the end. Take the 50 cm (20 in) strip of polyester satin ribbon. Hold it with the wrong side towards you and begin to roll it tightly from the right hand end, turning the top corner in first. Roll about six times. Using the cotton with the knot in the end, secure the bottom of the roll with a few stitches. Now fold the length of ribbon, bringing the satin side to the front, making the fold from the top edge. At the same time, roll the roll into the fold, taking care to keep the bottom of the rose even. Take a firm stitch at the base to secure this next step. Continue in this manner of folding the ribbon each time and rolling it onto the rose—the ribbon will alternate between the right and the wrong sides. Take care that the points at the top of the fold are not lined up in rows—try to alternate them. Secure the bottom with each fold and roll. Don't be afraid to take a good big securing stitch into the bottom. If the stitches are kept too close to the bottom edge the rose will fall apart. It is better to take the stitch about a third of the way up the rose as you progress towards the end. Use all 50 cm (20 in) of ribbon. Fold the tail end under and stitch it to the base. Leave the thread hanging, as it can be rethreaded and used for attaching the rose to the sloppy joe. Prepare all the roses you require (approximately eleven). To make up the design, determine a line or fold the sloppy joe down the centre front for placement of design.

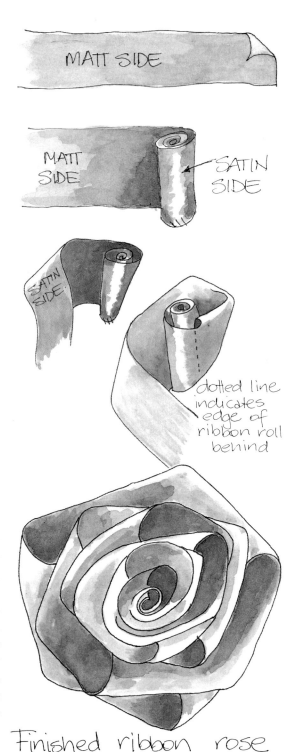

MATT SIDE

MATT SIDE — SATIN SIDE

SATIN SIDE

dotted line indicates edge of ribbon roll behind

Finished ribbon rose

The Pot

Cut the shape of the pot out of a strong piece of paper and place cut out shape in centre of the pot fabric on the wrong side. Trim the fabric around the pot shape leaving an excess of approximately 1 cm (3/8 in). Fold the excess fabric to the inside over the paper all round and tack it in place. Press with a steam iron. Remove the tacking and paper. Place the base of the pot about 9 cm (3½ in) up from the top of the basque band in the middle of the sloppy joe. Pin the pot in place.

The Stem

Take the length of fabric for the stem and place it on the sloppy joe, with the raw edge lying butted up against the centre front line or fold. The bottom end of the stem should lie about 1 cm (3/8 in) over the top of the pot — it will later be tucked under pot. Attach the stem to the sloppy joe by backstitching about 3 mm (1/8 in) from the raw edge, from the top of the stem to the level of the pot. Using a long, thin straight stick, such as a satay stick, roll the stem fabric tightly so that the finished roll lies over the centre front line. Pin the stem in place before removing the stick, and blind stitch down the edge of the roll with matching cotton. Tuck the base of the stalk under the pot and blind stitch round the edge of the pot in matching cotton.

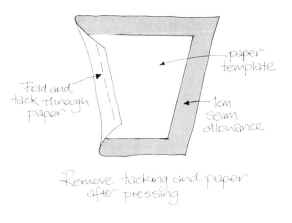

paper template

1cm seam allowance

Fold and tack through paper

Remove tacking and paper after pressing

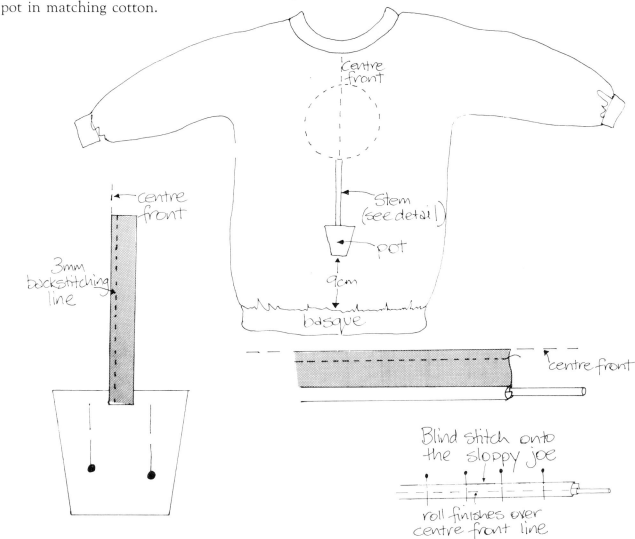

Centre front

Stem (see detail)

pot

9cm

basque

centre front

3mm backstitching line

centre front

Blind stitch onto the sloppy joe

roll finishes over centre front line

108

Lattice Work on the Pot

Thread a no. 3 straw needle and six strands of contrasting stranded cotton, about 1.3 m (1½ yds) long, and knot the end. Insert the needle into A from the wrong side of the sloppy joe. Take the needle down at B, up at C, down at D and so on, working alphabetically. At L, bring the needle up right beside where you went down before proceeding to M. Take care not to pull the thread tightly—it is better to be on the loose side. Finish off the thread behind the work. Thread a no. 9 crewel needle with three strands of embroidery cotton with a knot in the end and work a cross stitch over each of the points where threads cross each other on the pot. Finish off behind.

To Assemble the Roses

Spread the sloppy joe out on a table and arrange the roses. The first rose is secured over the top of the stalk. Rethread the needle with cotton from the bottom of the rose and stitch it onto the sloppy joe from the wrong side. Sew on all the roses in the same way.

Ribbon Loops

Thread a no. 9 crewel needle with machine cotton. Cut a 35 cm (14 in) length of 3 mm (1/8 in) ribbon, and make two loops and two tails as shown in the diagrams. Make five loops in all and secure the loops at the base with a few stitches. Stitch the loops to the sloppy joe, tucking the base under a rose. These are placed at random inside the circle of roses.

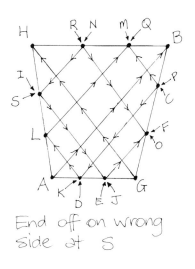

End off on wrong side at S

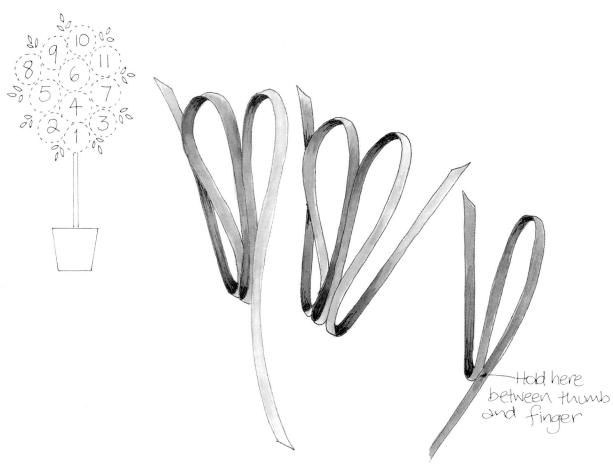

Hold here between thumb and finger

109

Leaves

Using a water-soluble pen, draw in the leaves in groups of three around the rose tree. Draw a vein down the middle of each leaf. Using three strands of embroidery cotton with a no. 9 crewel needle, work the leaves in fishbone stitch. Commence with small running stitches to the point of the leaf. Bring the needle up at A and down at B to right of line and up again at C to left of line. Now take the needle down at D and up at E. Repeat steps B and C and D and E until the leaf is filled in. Each stitch moves a little further down the leaf each time.

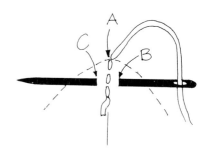

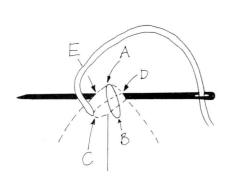 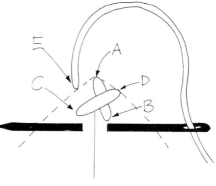

Bud

Cut a piece of 22 mm (7/8 in) width ribbon 4 cm (1½ in) long, and fold as shown in the diagram—A to C then B to C. With a needle and a thread with a knot in the end, gather the base of the bud and secure. Place the bud in position near the pot and oversew the base to the sloppy joe. With green cotton, work five or six long satin stitches from the centre of the base of the bud up the sides to hide the stitching. Work the stem in three strands and stem stitch. Work the leaves in fishbone stitch.

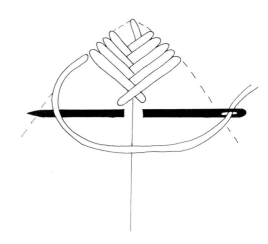

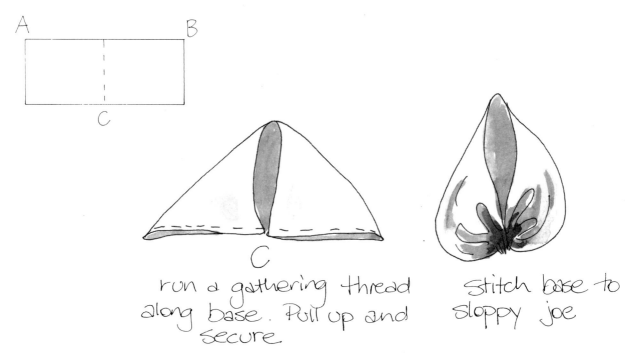

run a gathering thread along base. Pull up and secure.

stitch base to sloppy joe

17 Baby's Dress

Size
To fit baby six months old

Materials for dress
1.25 m (1 3/8 yds) x 115 cm (45 in) cotton voile
25 cm (3/8 yd) x 12 mm (½ in) lace insertion
1.5 m (1 5/8 yds) x 25 mm (1 in) lace insertion
3 m (3 3/8 yds) x 35 mm (1½ in) lace edging
2 m (2 ¼ yds) x 15 mm (5/8 in) lace edging
2 m (2 ¼ yds) x 6 mm (¼ in) polyester satin ribbon
1 m (1 1/8 yds) x 12 mm (½ in) beading
1.2 m (1¼ yds) entredeux or veining
2 buttons 8 mm (3/8 in) diameter
Stranded cottons of your choice
No. 9 crewel needle
Water-soluble fabric marking pen

New Stitches and Techniques
Pin tucks
French hand sewing
Using a basic pattern
Placket

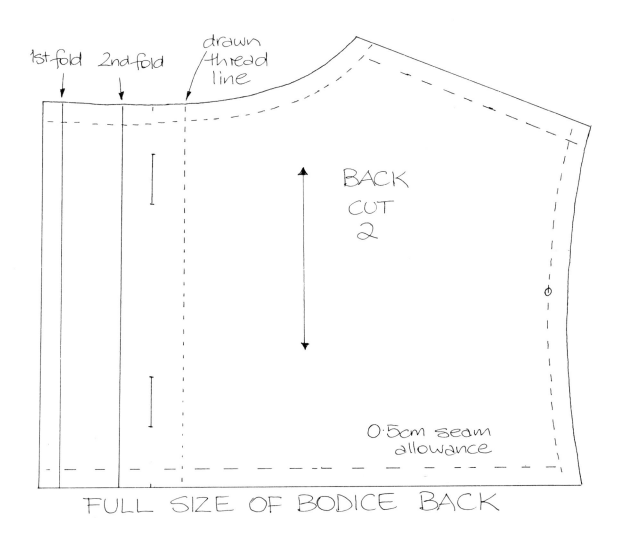

FULL SIZE OF BODICE BACK

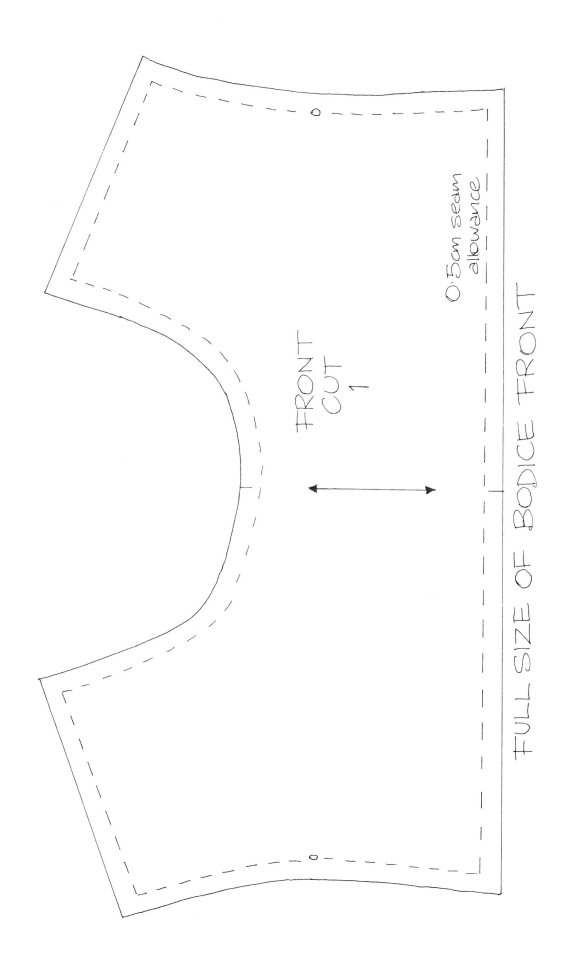

FRONT
CUT
1

0.5cm seam
allowance

FULL SIZE OF BODICE FRONT

113

Materials for Slip

1 m (1 1/8 yds) x 115 cm (45 in) cotton voile
1.5 m (1 5/8 yds) x 35 mm (1½ in) lace edging
50 cm (5/8 yd) narrow lace edging
2 buttons 8 mm (3/8 in) diameter

This dress is designed to fit a six months old child, but the same technique may be applied to any size, just adjust material requirements accordingly. The dress is quite a major undertaking, as it is practically all done by hand and takes considerable time, patience and skill—it's not for beginners. The most important technique used here is rolling and whipping. Once you have mastered this you should have no problems. To make a similar dress for a larger child, you could apply these techniques to a commercial pattern, but trim the seam allowances back to 5 mm (¼ in) or use a size smaller pattern than you usually would, as the hand-sewing techniques require smaller seam allowances.

Make up the pattern pieces but do not cut out the fabric yet. Draw threads to make sure the grain of the fabric is quite straight. Cut a rectangle of voile 15 x 24 cm (6 x 9½ in), which is larger than the yoke pattern piece. Fold the rectangle in half, short sides together, and mark the fold with a line of tacking or press it lightly with the iron. Centre the embroidery design at the middle of the fold and trace. Work the embroidery as indicated on the diagram, using a single thread of stranded cotton and a no. 9 crewel needle.

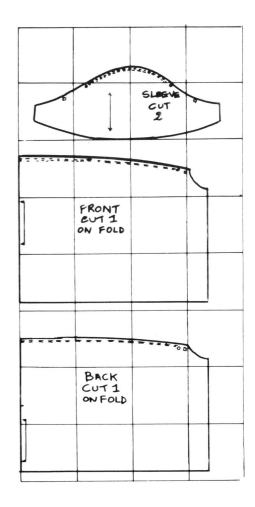

1 square = 10 cm

0.5 cm seam allowance

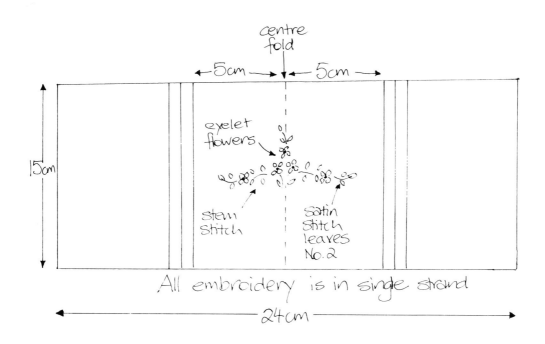

114

Pin Tucks

Measure 5 cm (2 in) from the centre front fold towards the edges and draw a thread. Fold the fabric along the drawn thread. Using a no. 9 crewel needle and machine cotton with a knot in the end of the thread, bring the needle up into the fold of the pin tuck. Work a row of small running stitches approximately a needle width below the fold through both layers of fabric. This forms a pin tuck. Measure 8 mm (3/8 in) from the stitching on the first pin tuck towards the outer edge, pull another thread, and work a pin tuck. Repeat once more. Work a total of three pin tucks. Note that 2 mm (1/16 in) is taken up with each pin tuck.

Now measure 1 cm (3/8 in) from the stitching on the last pin tuck, draw a thread and cut along the drawn thread. (Reserve the cut piece of fabric.) Place the right sides of the fabric and the narrow insertion lace together. Pin the insertion into place first below the cut edge of fabric and roll and whip the insertion to the fabric. It is important to pin the insertion to help prevent any stretching that might otherwise occur. Place the piece of fabric that was previously cut off with its right side against the right side of the other side of the insertion, pin, and then roll and whip as before.

Measure 8 mm (3/8) in from the edge of the insertion and draw a thread. Work two pin tucks in the manner already described. There will be five pin tucks in all on half the yoke. Work the other side of the yoke to correspond.

Rinse out the water-soluble pen markings in cold water. Once you have completed the embroidery, insertion and pin tucks, press and lay flat. Press the pin tucks out towards the edge on both sides of the centre front. Centre the yoke pattern piece and trace around the outside edges with the water-soluble pen. Machine around the outline with quite small stitches before trimming the fabric back, right to the line of machine stitching, so that the stitching will be right on the edge of the bodice fabric.

Cut out the rest of the pieces for the dress.

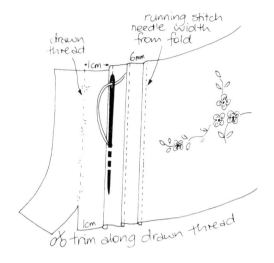

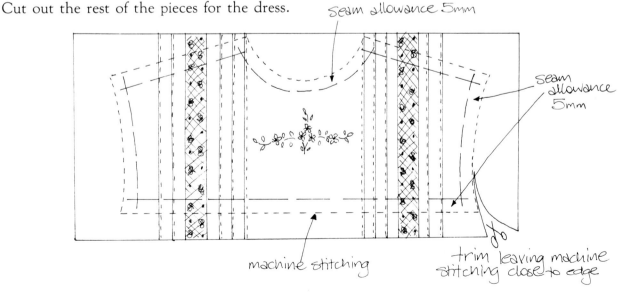

Yoke Back

Draw a thread on the raw edge of the back opening and trim to straighten edge of fabric. Measure in 4.5 cm (1¾ in) from the raw edge and draw four to six threads. On the back opening, turn the raw edge in for 5 mm (¼ in) to wrong side and press. Fold the back opening right sides together along the fold line and stitch the top and bottom of the fold 5 mm (¼ in) in from the raw edges on the seam allowance. Turn the folded band right sides out and tack along the folded edge so that it lies right beside the drawn threads. Hemstitch on the hemstitch line, catching the back opening band in at the same time on the wrong side of the work (see baby's nightgown). Sew the shoulder seams together with a VERY fine french seam. You only have 5 mm (¼ in) seam allowance.

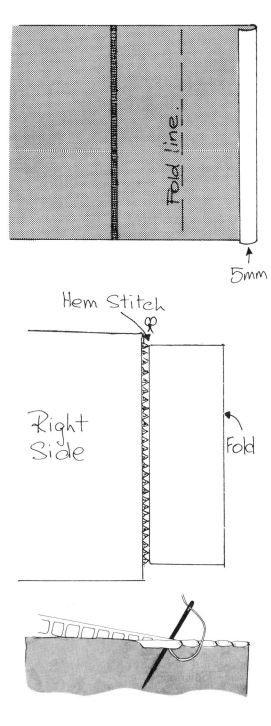

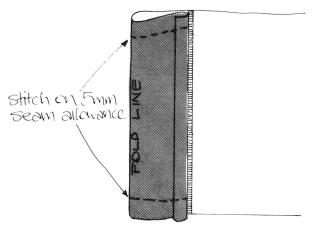

Neck Edge

Roll and whip the entredeux or veining to the machined neck edge, right sides together. Whip the 15 mm (5/8 in) lace edging to the veining (RIGHT sides together) using gathering method no. 1 (see the sachet for this method). Instead of veining, a beading could be substituted and a ribbon later threaded through it. Finish off the lace edges at the back with a small double hem.

Yoke Bottom

Roll and whip the beading onto the front and back, with the right sides together. Double hem the two edges of beading lace at centre back.

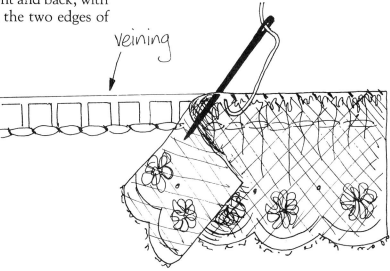

The Skirt

Find the centre front of the skirt and centre the embroidery design on the skirt and trace. Embroider the design to match the yoke.

To make the placket in the skirt back, fold the skirt in half and make a 12 cm (5 in) cut down the centre back fold. Cut a straight strip of voile 26 x 4 cm (10 x 1½ in). Place the right side of the strip to the right side of skirt and machine stitch 4 mm (¼ in) from the edge, tapering off to nothing at the bottom. Leave the needle in the fabric. Pivot the fabric and sew back up to the top of the placket from nothing to 4 mm (¼ in). Press the seams towards the centre. Fold in 5 mm (¼ in) on the strip, press and fold again. Blind hem the strip to the skirt, catching the fold into the back of the machine stitches. Fold the right side of the placket under, so that the seam is on the fold, turn in the raw edges at the top of the placket and tack across the top.

French seam the front and back skirts together at the sides. Run a machine stitch around the very edge of the skirt armhole. This will leave a 5 mm (¼ in) seam allowance for rolling and whipping. This can be done in two ways, but be careful NOT TO GATHER THE PLACKET.

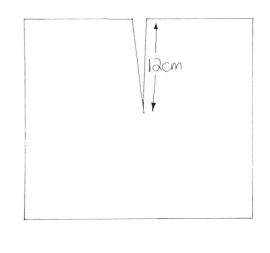

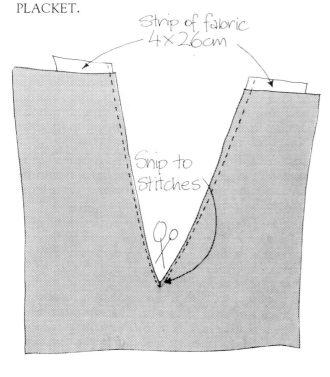

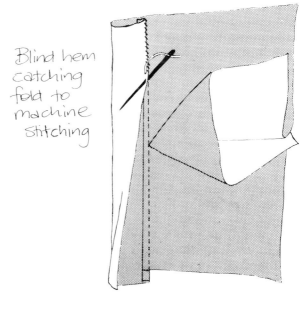

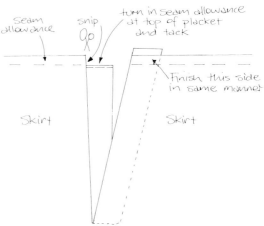

117

1. Roll and whip the top of the skirt with large stitches. Every few stitches pull the thread tight, gathering the fabric along the way.
2. Turn the fabric under about 5 mm (¼ in) and work two or three rows of small gathering stitches. These will remain visible so make them neat. At the end, pull the threads to gather up the fabric.

Whichever method you use, gather the fabric up to fit the yoke. Do not end off the gathering threads at this stage, as you may need to adjust them.

With the right sides together, whip the gathered edge of the skirt onto the bottom edge of the beading lace at the waist of the back and front yokes with small firm stitches.

The skirt bottom is worked by rolling and whipping the 25 mm (1 in) lace insertion on, with the right sides together. Join the lace at centre back. The 35 mm (1½ in) lace edging is then whipped and gathered to the insertion, right sides together. Join the lace at centre back.

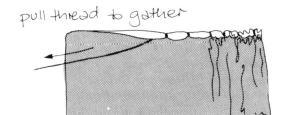

Method 1

pull thread to gather

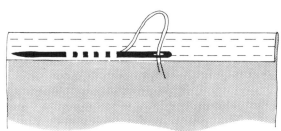

Method 2

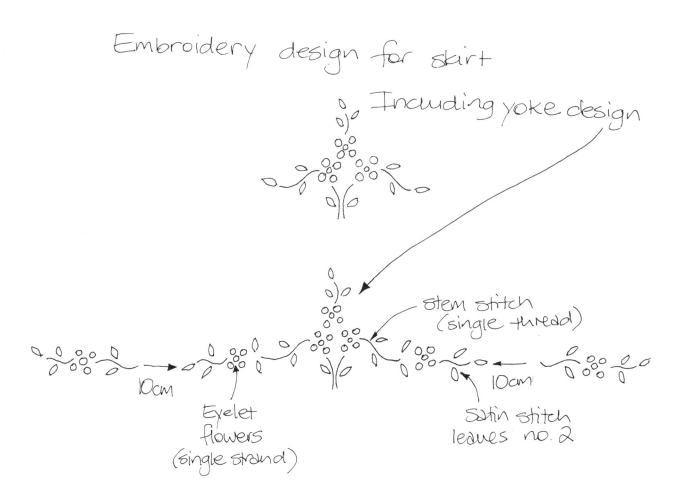

Embroidery design for skirt

Including yoke design

Stem stitch (single thread)

10cm

Eyelet flowers (single strand)

10cm

Satin stitch leaves no. 2

118

Sleeves

Sew the underarm seam with a fine french seam. Roll and gather all round the bottom of the sleeve until it measures about 16 cm (6½ in). Whip the lace beading to the bottom of the sleeve, right sides together, joining the ends at the underarm seam. Whip and gather the 12 mm (½ in) lace edging to the other side of the beading, joining the edges at the underarm seam. Roll and gather the head of the sleeve between the notches, leaving the thread hanging for adjusting later. Using a separate thread, roll and whip the rest of the raw edge of the sleeve, *without* gathering.

Roll and whip the veining to the armhole edge of the bodice, joining the lace at the underarm seam. Adjust the sleeve gathers to fit the armhole and whip the rolled edge of the sleeve to the veining on the armhole edge of the bodice right sides together, matching the notches.

Buttonholes

Work two buttonholes on the right hand band of the bodice back. Thread ribbons through the lace beading.

Slip

Cut out the pattern pieces for the slip using the front and back yokes and skirt front and back of the dress, but do NOT cut out sleeves.

Join the front and back yokes at the shoulder seams with french seams. Sew the side seams of skirt together with french seams. Blind hem the back yoke opening. Make a placket in the centre back of the skirt. Gather the slip skirt at the waist using either method 1 or 2. Roll and whip the yoke bottom and join it to the skirt at the same time, right sides together. Roll and whip the sleeve edges of the bodice. Lace may be added at the same time but is not necessary. The neck edge may also be finished with a rolled and whipped edge, joining in a narrow lace if desired. Work buttonholes and sew on the buttons. Roll and whip the hem of the slip, and attach the lace at the same time without gathering it.

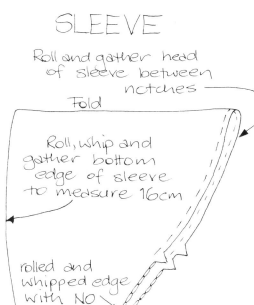

SLEEVE

Roll and gather head of sleeve between notches —

Fold

Roll, whip and gather bottom edge of sleeve to measure 16cm

rolled and whipped edge with NO gathering

Narrow french seam

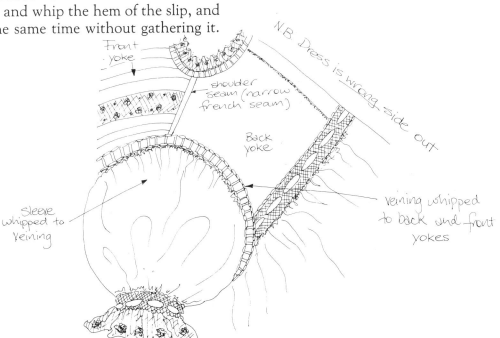

Front yoke

shoulder seam (narrow french seam)

N.B. Dress is wrong side out

Back yoke

sleeve whipped to veining

veining whipped to back and front yokes

18 Nightgown

Size 83–92 cm (32–36 in)

Materials

2.5 m (2¾ yds) x 115 cm (45 in) cotton voile
3.2 m (3½ yds) x 20 mm (¾ in) insertion lace
4.5 m (5 yds) x 5 cm (2 in) edging lace
2 m (2 1/8 yds) x 15 mm (5/8 in) edging lace
1 m (1 yd) x 10 mm (3/8 in) OR
50 cm (5/8 yd) x 20 mm (¾ in) beading
1.5 m (1 5/8 yds) ribbon to fit beading
Water-soluble fabric marking pen
Stranded cottons (your choice of colours)
No. 9 crewel needle

For my trousseau my mother made for me a beautiful night-
gown, which I treasure and still have to this day. Here is
a copy of that nightgown. It is definitely not a project for
the faint-hearted or the novice, but if you have worked your
way through this book you should have no problems at all.
I know you will love the end result.

New Stitches and Techniques

French hand sewing
Whipping lace together

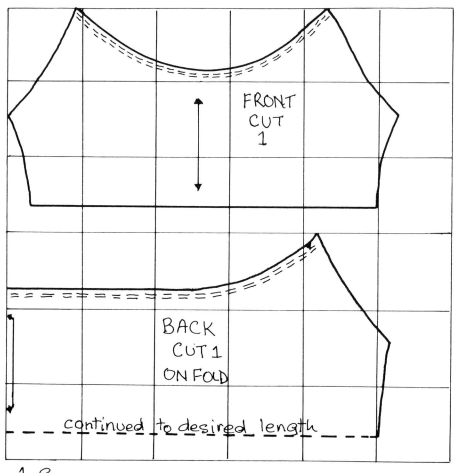

FRONT
CUT
1

BACK
CUT 1
ON FOLD

continued to desired length

1 Square = 10 cm
1 cm seam allowance

The size of the nightdress is easily adjusted over the sizes specified by altering the amount of gathering and lengthening or shortening the shoulder straps. The pattern could also be adjusted for a larger size by slashing twice through the bodice patterns, to divide them into equal thirds, and moving the edge pieces outwards. (The strips of voile used for the bodice will also have to be a little wider.) Lengthen the front bodice a little and cut the bias strip for the shoulder straps longer too.

The Front Bodice

Cut a strip of voile 20 x 28 cm (8 x 11 in). Fold the two 20 cm (8 in) ends together and mark the fold. This will be the centre front. Now measure 19 mm (¾ in) to each side of the centre fold and draw a thread. Fold the fabric along the drawn thread line and work a pin tuck the width of your needle. Work the pin tuck by hand with small running stitches. You will now have a panel in the centre front with a pin tuck on each side. Measure 12 mm (½ in) from the stitching on the pin tuck out towards the edges, draw a thread and work another pin tuck. Repeat this step once more so you will have a panel with three pin tucks on each side. Next measure 17 mm (5/8 in) outside the last pin tuck, draw a thread, and cut along line of drawn threads.

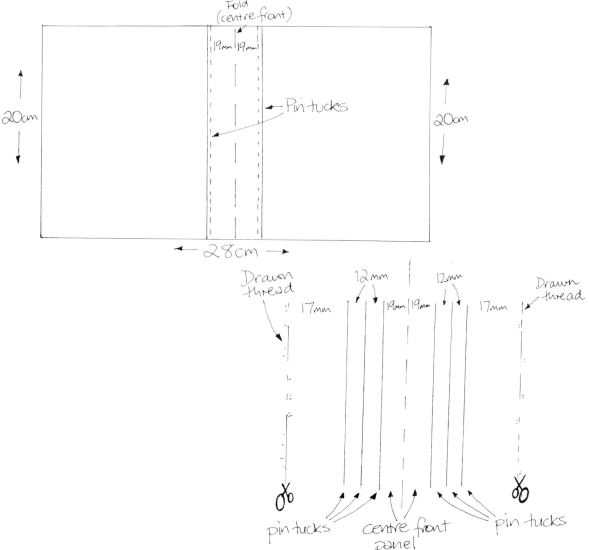

Pattern match the design on the insertion before cutting two lengths 20 cm (8 in) long. Pin one piece to each side of the voile with RIGHT sides together and roll and whip the insertion lace to the edge of the voile. If the insertion is pinned first it will help prevent stretching of either the insertion or the voile.

Now cut two pieces of voile 27 x 16 cm (10½ x 6½ in). Pin one piece to each side of the voile panel, RIGHT sides together, aligning the bottom edges. You will notice your new voile strips are longer than the central panel—this is to allow for the neck curve. Roll and whip the voile to the insertion lace. Measure 12 mm (½ in) from the insertion into each of the new voile panels and work a pin tuck. Repeat pin tucks until there are three on both sides. Leave another plain panel measuring 38 mm (1½ in) before drawing a thread and working three more equidistant pin tucks. Leave 17 mm (5/8 in) outside these pin tucks, draw a thread and cut the fabric. Once again, pattern match the insertion lace before cutting two pieces 27 cm (10½ in) long. Pin the RIGHT sides together on each side of the front panel and roll and whip together.

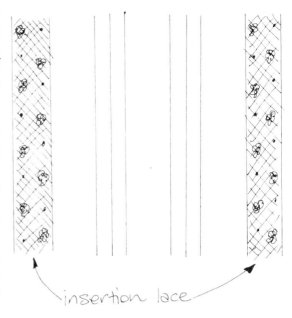

insertion lace

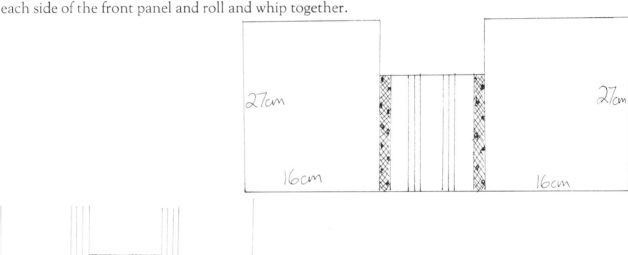

27cm

16cm

27cm

16cm

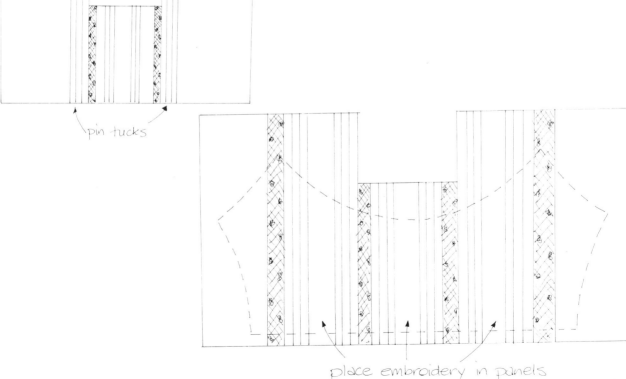

pin tucks

place embroidery in panels

122

Cut two more panels of voile 10 x 27 cm (4 x 10½ in). Attach one panel to each side of the central panel, RIGHT sides together, by rolling and whipping. Press the front panel, pressing the pin tucks out towards the edges of each of the panels. Prepare the bodice pattern pieces.

Lie the paper pattern guide for the front onto the front panel and trace around the outside with a water-soluble pen. Machine stitch twice over the traced line to hold all the stitching before cutting. Make sure when stitching that you keep all the pin tucks going in the right direction.

Next embroider the three plain panels on front, tracing the design onto the fabric first. Flowers are worked with eyelets in the centre (see the technique under the half slip). The leaves are worked in satin stitch no. 2 (see collars). Dots are worked in satin stitch (see the shoe bag). All the embroidery is worked in single thread. Once the embroidery is completed rinse in cold water to remove the pen markings, dry and press.

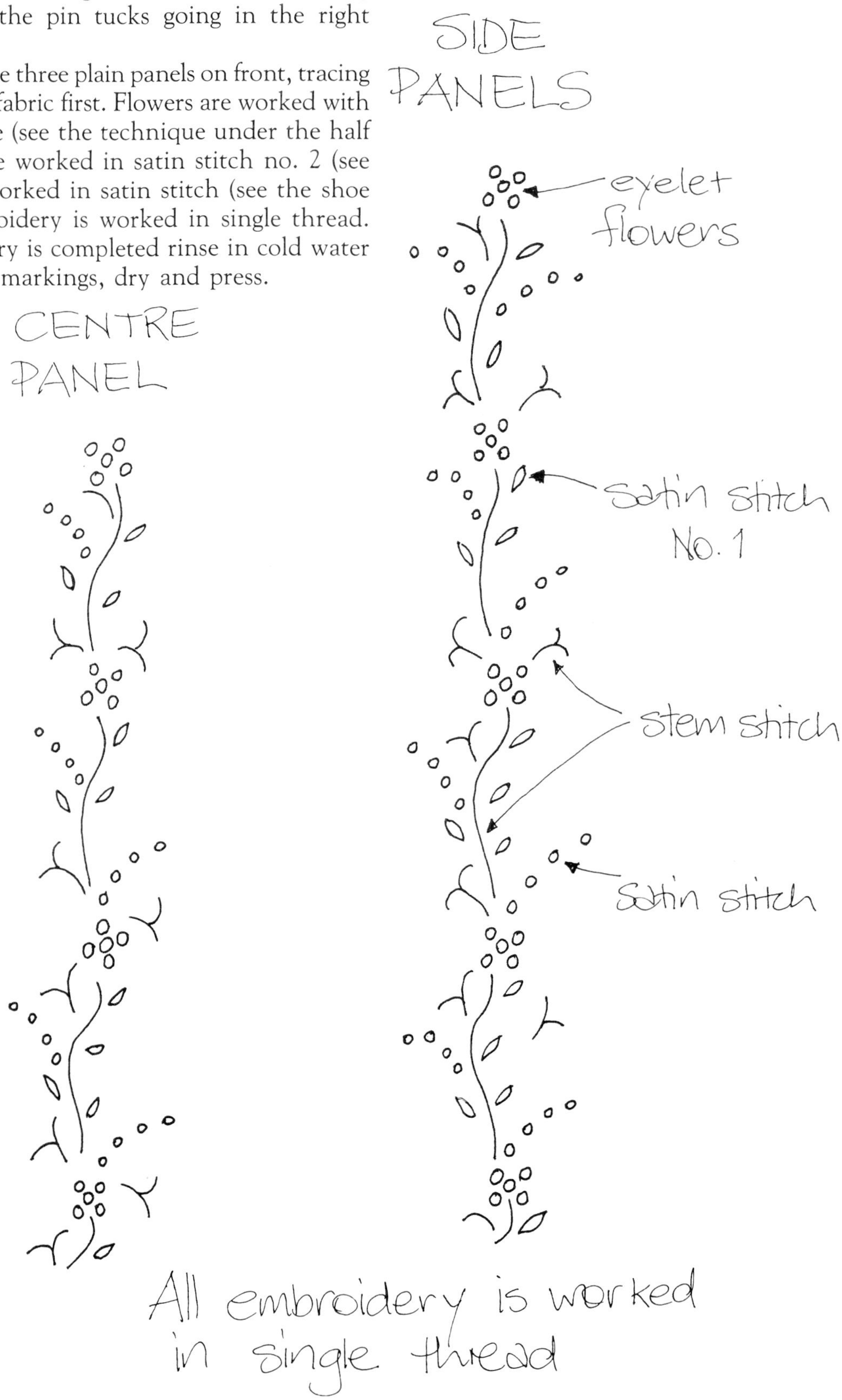

SIDE PANELS

— eyelet flowers

satin stitch No. 1

stem stitch

satin stitch

CENTRE PANEL

All embroidery is worked in single thread

Trim away the raw edges all round the front panel, leaving the machine stitching on the edge of the bodice. Cut a length of beading a little longer than necessary and pin, RIGHT sides together, to the bottom of the front panel. Roll and whip into place. If you are using broderie beading you may need to trim away the raw edge of the fabric from the beading before joining it to the front panel. If you are using a wide beading insertion (2 cm or ¾ in) it will be sufficient to have one piece of insertion beading. You could, however, have two 1 cm (3/8 in) strips of beading insertion instead, in which case they will need to be whipped together first.

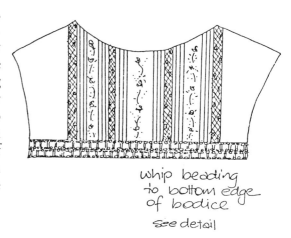

whip beading
to bottom edge
of bodice
see detail

Whipping Lace Together

Trim the fabric away from the edge of broderie beading, if there is a fabric edge, and place the RIGHT sides of the two pieces of beading together. Whip the two edges together, taking the needle through both edges of beading every 1 to 2 mm (1/16 in). The thread goes over the top of the two edges as in overcasting. Keep the tension firm.

To Attach the Skirt

Cut the skirt 1 m (1 yd) wide and 87 cm (34 in) long (or the length desired). There are several methods of attaching the skirt to the bodice.

1. Turn a small double hem to the wrong side of the skirt and work two rows of running stitches from one end to the other, one row at each fold. These stitches will be left in place so make them even. Pull the two threads from both ends to form gathers. Ease the gathers to fit the fullness of the skirt to the bottom of the beading, and with RIGHT sides together pin in place before whipping them very firmly together (see the baby's dress for this technique).

2. Turn a single hem approximately 1 cm (3/8 in) in depth and follow method no. 1, but work three rows of running stitches. The raw edges are quite stable as they are firmly gathered.

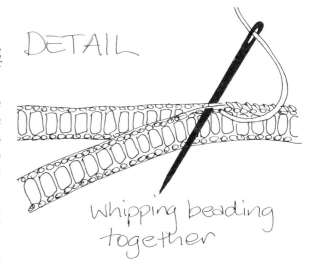

DETAIL

Whipping beading
together

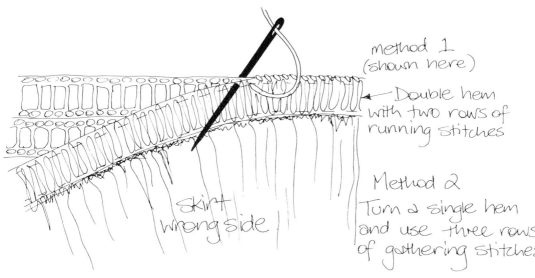

Skirt
wrong side

method 1
(shown here)
Double hem
with two rows of
running stitches

Method 2
Turn a single hem
and use three rows
of gathering stitches

125

3. Roll the skirt edge to the wrong side of fabric and whip with long stitches, pushing the fabric along the whipping stitches to form gathers every 4–5 cm (1½–2 in). Ease the gathers to fit the beading insertion. With RIGHT sides together, pin, then whip firmly into place.

Cut out the back of the nightgown using the back bodice pattern for the top and cutting the length to match that of the front bodice plus beading plus skirt from the underarm. Join it to the front at the sides with fine french seams. Run a stay stitch all round the armhole 1 cm (3/8 in) in from the edge. Bind the armhole edge with a voile bias binding, keeping it neat and fine (see the baby's nightgown for the technique).

Gather the back neck edge between the notches. Pull the gathers until the back neck measures about 38 cm (15 in). Gather the front bodice and ease it very slightly to measure about 38–39 cm (15–15½ in).

Make a long bias strip in voile measuring about 115 cm (45 in) long and 2.5 cm (1 in) wide. With the RIGHT sides together, place the bias strip against the neck edge of the nightgown, commencing at one shoulder on the back. Pin across the back from one end to the other. Leave a section measuring about 16.5 cm (6½ in) for the shoulder strap and continue pinning across the front of the bodice, again leaving 16.5 cm (6½ in) for the second shoulder strap at the other end. Join the shoulder strap with the back binding. Try the nightgown on at this stage, before any machining is done, in case the shoulder straps need adjusting. Machine the bias binding to the front and back of the nightgown using a 1 cm (3/8 in) seam allowance. Trim the raw edges to 5 mm (¼ in). Double fold the bias to the inside of the nightgown and hem into the machine stitches on the wrong side. The finished bias binding should be no wider than 5 mm (¼ in). Trim and fold the bias on the shoulder straps to match the neck edges and oversew the folded edges very finely together.

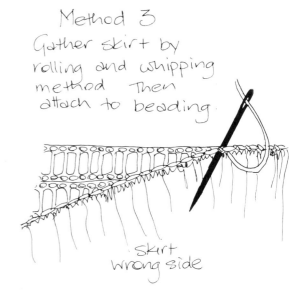

Method 3
Gather skirt by rolling and whipping method Then attach to beading.

skirt
wrong side

gather between notches

bind armholes with voile bias binding

slightly gathered and ease front neckline

french seams at sides

To attach the 15 mm (5/8 in) lace around the neck edge of the nightgown, place the right sides of the fabric and lace together, commence at the back, and whip the lace onto the bias binding, gathering at same time (see the sachet for the technique). Gather and whip simultaneously the wider lace (5 cm or 2 in) to the shoulder strap on the sleeve edge. Leave a tail of lace at both ends to be later hemmed and joined to the armhole. Attach a second row of the wider lace (5 cm or 2 in), again leaving a tail at both ends for joining. To attach the second row of lace, pin the straight edge of lace underneath the scalloped edge of the first piece of lace. Join with a fine running stitch through both pieces of lace, working a back stitch every three or four stitches. This forms a cap sleeve. Make a narrow double hem in the laces at the armhole edges and hem them neatly inside the bindings.

Nightgown Hem

Three methods can be used to hem the nightgown:
1. shell edging (see the camisole for the technique),
2. a narrow hem, finished with blind hemming (see the baby's nightgown), or
3. roll and whip the insertion lace, RIGHT sides together, around the bottom edge. Then whip on the edging lace, RIGHT sides together, gathering at the same time (see the sachet for this technique). Enough lace edging and insertion is included in the list of materials for hemming the nightgown.

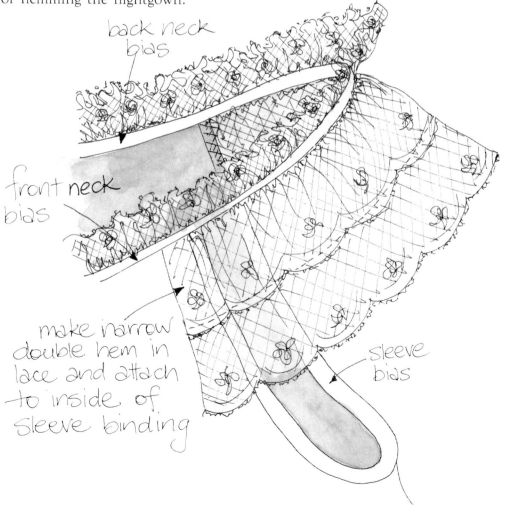

19 Decorative Beaded Ornament

Materials

12 cm (5 in) x 90 cm (36 in) velveteen
1 skein perle cotton no. 5 OR
2 skeins stranded cotton to match velveteen
Assorted beads: diamantés, pearls, glass beads, drop pearls
Matching machine cottons
Long needle with large eye (about 9 cm or 3½ in)
Beading needle or no. 9 straw needle, chenille needle
Dacron filling
Fine crochet hook

This funny little bejewelled ornament is great fun to make and may be used for a number of different purposes. It is just the right size to hang on the end of a light cord or a curtain pull. Another idea is to hang it from a key on an antique cupboard or anywhere you would have a tassel. The colour and design you choose will probably be determined by the purpose you have in mind. I have included three different designs here for you to choose from or perhaps you would like to create your own.

New Stitches and Techniques

Beading
Tassel
Twisted cord

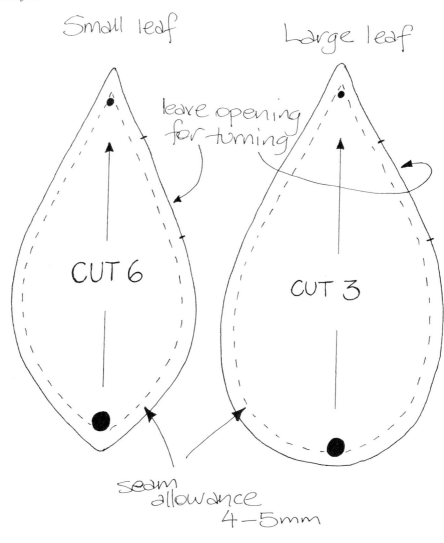

Small leaf

Large leaf

leave opening for turning

CUT 6

CUT 3

seam allowance 4—5mm

128

Begin by cutting out the shapes. When working with velveteen, the nap must run the same way, so keep this in mind when cutting out: the points of the arrows must all go in the same direction. Cut six small leaf shapes and three large leaf shapes. Transfer the markings from one of the diagrams onto three of the small leaf shapes. Bead and embroider according to the diagram or choose your own design using whatever beads you have. Keep the decoration within the seam allowance.

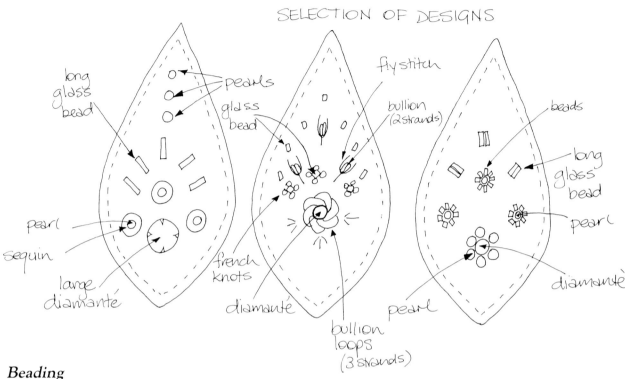

SELECTION OF DESIGNS

Beading

Beads are attached to the fabric using a double thread of machine cotton and a backstitch. As this ornament could be handled quite a lot, it would be advisable to work each of the larger beads with two stitches through the middle for security. To commence, bring the knotted thread through from the back of the work, just to one side of the position for the first bead at A. Thread the bead onto the needle, push the needle back down again on the other side of the bead at B, and bring the needle back up again at A. Take the needle through the bead a second time and go back down at B. This double stitching is only necessary if the ornament is going to be handled continuously. If it is purely for decoration, one stitch will be sufficient. Continue adding beads in this manner, finishing each flower off on the back of the work with a few backstitches.

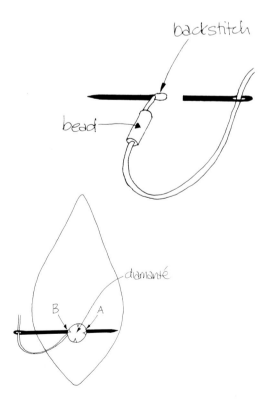

129

Making Up the Ornament

With RIGHT sides together, sew one beaded shape to one unbeaded shape on the machine, leaving an opening in the upper side for turning. The seam allowance is 4–5 mm (¼ in). Trim across the point at the top and bottom and nick seam allowance on the curves. Turn right side out, and overcast the opening together with matching machine cotton. Make up the three beaded shapes in this manner.

Now take the three large leaf shapes and, with RIGHT sides together, sew the three shapes together from the small dot to the large dot, leaving an opening for turning. Turn right sides out and fill with dacron stuffing, filling very firmly. Close the opening with overcasting.

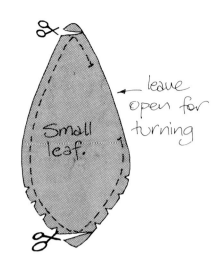

leave open for turning

Small leaf.

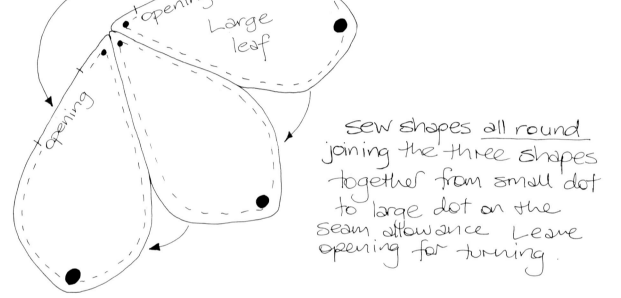

opening

Large leaf

opening

opening

sew shapes all round joining the three shapes together from small dot to large dot on the seam allowance. Leave opening for turning.

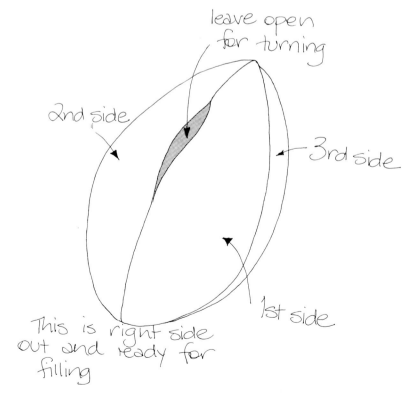

leave open for turning

2nd side

3rd side

1st side

This is right side out and ready for filling

Take two of the beaded shapes and, with RIGHT sides together, oversew from A to B with machine thread doubled. Leave an opening at B, its size depending on the size of the cord to be used. If you are going to use cord for a light pull, the opening will need to be large enough to accommodate this. If you are using the cord suggested here, the opening is very small indeed, so close the seam at B to within about 2 mm (1/8 in) of B. Next, sew the third beaded shape to the other two in the same manner with right sides together. Turn the beaded shape right side out.

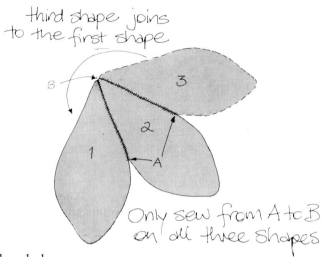

third shape joins to the first shape

Only sew from A to B on all three shapes

Beading the Sides

To commence beading down the sides of the beaded shape, start with a matching double thread, knotted in the end. Begin at the top and bring the needle up from the inside about 4 mm (1/8 in) from B. Thread a long glass bead onto the needle and backstitch it into place. Repeat beading until point C is reached. When point C is reached, change beads to round glass beads and back stitch those along seam line. When point A is reached, attach a drop pearl. Continue in this manner till all three sides and points are beaded.

Bead the large shape with long glass beads along the seam lines around the bottom and up the sides as far as X, or about 6 cm (2½ in).

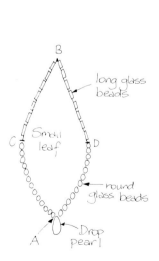

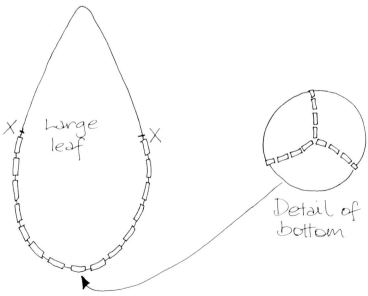

Detail of bottom

Tassel

Cut a length of cardboard about 6 x 6 cm (2½ x 2½ in). Wind perle cotton or six strands of stranded cotton around the cardboard about forty to fifty times. Thread a needle with a 30 cm (12 in) length of the same cotton, placing the two ends of thread through the eye of the needle to form a loop at the other end. Pass the point of the needle along the top edge of the cardboard between the cardboard and the threads and back through the loop in the cotton. Now cut the threads along the bottom edge of the cardboard. Pull the loop, holding the threads taut, and feed the needle down into the tassel. Pull the thread tight and remove the needle. Trim the thread level with the bottom of the tassel.

Thread a needle with perle or stranded cotton in the same manner, using a length of thread about 60 cm (24 in) long. Place a small ball of cotton wool into the head of the tassel, secure the threads beneath with another looped thread and pull tightly. Take the needle up through the head of the tassel and out the top. These two threads will be used later, so do not cut them off.

Now thread a needle with a 1 m (1 yd) length of perle cotton or three strands of stranded cotton. Knot the end and bring the needle up through the tassel to the head once again, so that the knot is hidden within. Commence blanket stitching around the head of the tassel, keeping the cotton wool tucked into the middle as you go. After the first circle of blanket stitching is completed, take the needle into the stitch from the previous round each time you make a new blanket stitch. When working the final round of blanket stitch, include the looped thread holding the tassel at the base.

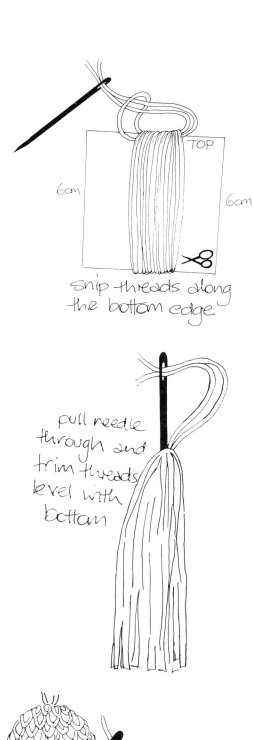

snip threads along the bottom edge

pull needle through and trim threads level with bottom

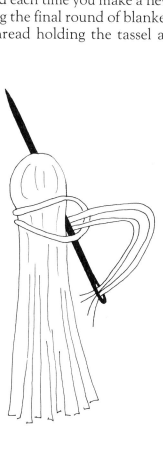

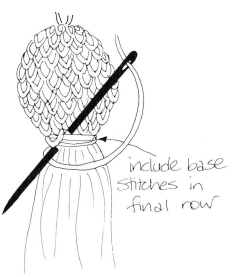

include base stitches in final row

133

To Complete the Ornament

Take the two long threads protruding from the head of the tassel and thread them through the eye of a long needle. Put the point of the needle in at the junction of the three seams at the bottom of the large leaf shape. Pass the point of the needle through and out the point of the leaf shape and pull through. Separate the two threads from the tassel and secure each one separately to the point of the large leaf shape, keeping the tension on the tassel taut, so it lies firmly in place.

If this ornament is to be used on a light cord or curtain pull, now is the time to attach the end of cord. Hook and pull the cord through the hole in the top of the beaded section and stitch it very firmly into place at the point of the large velvet shape. Slide the beaded section onto the large leaf section, matching the seam lines with the long glass beads. To hold it in place, use a matching cotton, and secure the light cord to the top of ornament. Hide the stitching with a few circles of perle cotton, the ends of which are taken back down under beaded section and trimmed off out of sight.

Twisted Cord

Take a length of perle cotton or six strands of stranded cotton 115 cm (45 in) long. Knot both ends together and loop the knotted end over a hook or door knob. Slip a pencil into the loop at the other end and twist the pencil clockwise until the cotton is very well twisted. Place your finger in the mid-point of the twisted cotton. Bring both ends of the twisted cotton together and allow it to twist up and form a twisted cord. Slip the end off the hook and cut the knot from the end of cord. Thread this end of the cord through a needle with a large eye, such as a chenille needle and knot the other end of the cord with a strong knot. Take a stitch through the top end of the large shape so that the knotted end of the cord is secured. Take one more stitch, remove the needle, and knot the other end of the cord securely, leaving a loop of twisted cord. Pull the cord in the middle so that you can test the strength of the knots in the two ends of cord.

Poke a fine crochet hook through the hole in the top of the small beaded section, hook the twisted cord attached to the large shape, and pull the cord through the hole. Slide the top beaded shape over the large bottom shape, matching the seams with long glass beads. Pull securely into place and tie a knot in the twisted cord to lie directly on top of small beaded shape. You are now finished and I hope you are well pleased with the result.

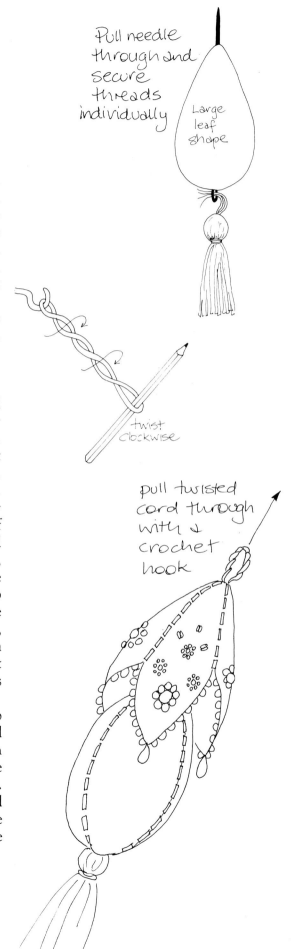

Pull needle through and secure threads individually

Large leaf shape

twist clockwise

pull twisted cord through with a crochet hook

20 Beaded Sweater

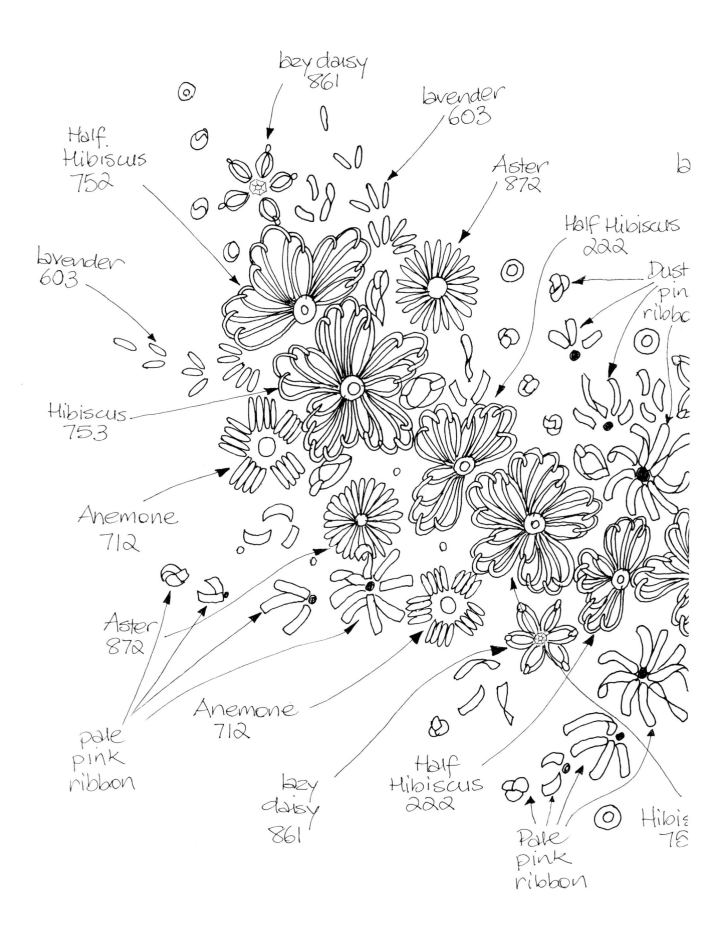

lazy daisy
861

Half.
Hibiscus
752

lavender
603

lavender
603

Aster
872

b

Half Hibiscus
222

Dust
pin
ribbo

Hibiscus
753

Anemone
712

Aster
872

pale
pink
ribbon

Anemone
712

lazy
daisy
861

Half
Hibiscus
222

Pale
pink
ribbon

Hibi
7E

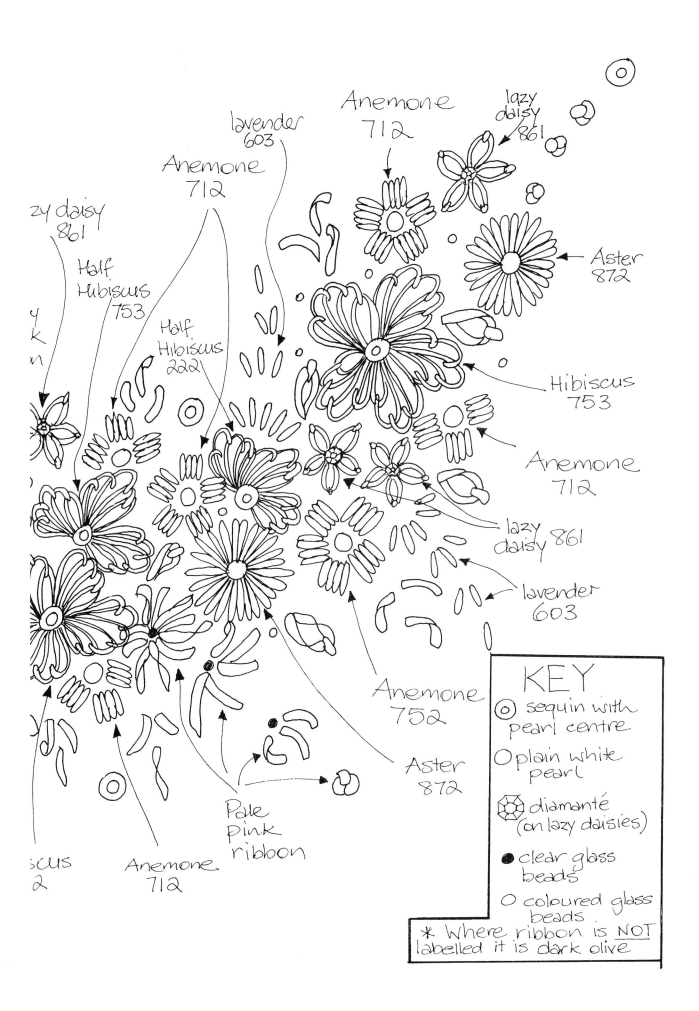

lavender
603

Anemone
712

Anemone
712

lazy
daisy
861

zy daisy
861

Half
Hibiscus
753

Half
Hibiscus
2221

Aster
872

Hibiscus
753

Anemone
712

lazy
daisy 861

lavender
603

Anemone
752

Aster
872

Pale
Pink
ribbon

scus
2

Anemone
712

KEY

- ⊚ sequin with pearl centre
- ○ plain white pearl
- ⬡ diamanté (on lazy daisies)
- ● clear glass beads
- ○ coloured glass beads

* Where ribbon is NOT labelled it is dark olive

Materials

1 finely knitted sweater
Crewel wool. Suggested colours: Appletons nos 222, 603, 712, 752, 753, 861, 872
3 m (3 3/8 yds) x 3 mm (1/8 in) green polyester satin ribbon *or* use crewel wool, Appletons no. 348
1 m (1 1/8 yds) x 3 mm (1/8 in) dark pink polyester satin ribbon
2 m (2 ¼ yds) x 3 mm (1/8 in) pale pink polyester satin ribbon
Beads, such as pearls, small and slightly larger
Silver and gold sequins, small diamantés
Selection of beads in clear or coloured glass
No. 18 chenille needle, no. 9 or 10 straw needle

If you enjoy wool embroidery this sweater is relatively fast to work, soft, pretty and very rewarding. The stitches are simple and have all been covered in the preceding chapters. The only difference here is the use of ribbon in the embroidery to add a different texture and dimension, and the beading, which is enormous fun to do and looks wonderful.

I simply began in the middle and worked out to either side, popping a daisy in here and a bit of lavender in there as the mood took me. I had the general idea that I would like to work in a semi-circle below the neck, but you may have a V-shaped or a boat neck, so your design will necessarily be different. I will describe to you the way I arrived at the finished design so that you can adapt your design in the same manner. I have given the flowers names for the sake of identification and have included the numbers of the Appletons crewel wool I used as a guide, but there are so many wonderful colours to choose from that even choosing the colours becomes an exciting part of the exercise. The sweater I worked on is a very pale peach colour and has a crew neck.

Commence by running a tacking thread in a coloured machine cotton following the line you would like your embroidery to take. This acts as a guide and will be removed when embroidery is completed. You will work the first flowers over the top of this tacking thread.

Hibiscus

There is no need to draw the design first. Begin the embroidery by working the large hibiscus, which is roughly in the bottom centre of the design. Mark the centre of the hibiscus with a pencil dot and, with two strands of wool, commence with a running stitch towards the centre of the flower so that the stitches will be hidden when the petal is worked over the top. Hold your work so that the centre of the flower is away from you and the petal to be worked is closest to you. Form a petal by working blanket stitch over the top of running stitches. Make the first a short stitch, the next one slightly longer, the third stitch longer again, then reverse, so stitches get shorter and shorter. Work five petals in total, leaving a small circle in the middle of the flower for beading later. Work a half hibiscus in the same manner with three petals only.

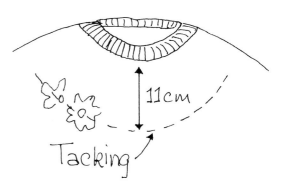

Tacking

11 cm

HIBISCUS

First petal of hibiscus worked in blanket stitch

138

Aster

The aster is worked in three strands of Appletons crewel wool. Secure the wool into the centre of the flower with a backstitch, then work in the straight stitches from the centre out in a circle, fanning the stitches out slightly at the outer edge of the circle. End off behind by darning the wool into the stitches at the back of the work.

Daisies

These are worked in two strands with five or six lazy daisy petals, leaving a small hole in the middle for a bead (see the crib blanket for the technique).

Anemone

The wool for the anemone may either be secured into some completed embroidery on the wrong side of the work or begin on the right side of the work by leaving a tail of wool that will darn it. Using two strands of wool, work four or five straight stitches next to each other in a straight line to form a petal. Work three to five petals on each flower depending on whether it is a whole or half flower. Again, leave a hole in the centre for a bead.

Lavender

Lavender is worked in three strands of wool in groups of straight stitches (see the crib blanket for the technique).

Ribbon

This narrow 3 mm (1/8 in) ribbon will thread through the eye of a chenille needle. I have used it like the wool. It doesn't matter if the ribbon twists, in fact it adds to the texture. The first stitch comes through from the wrong side, leaving a tail of ribbon at the back. Stitch the tail down with machine cotton later. Work the flowers in a series of straight stitches with the ribbon. The circular flowers begin in the centre and fan out towards the outer edges of the circle. The semi-circle flowers start at the centre and fan out, but have only three or four stitches. To finish off ribbon on the back of the work, use a no. 9 crewel needle threaded with machine cotton. Sew the tails of ribbon to another ribbon stitch on the back of the work with a few overcasting stitches until it is quite secure.

ASTER

straight stitches are fanned out in a circle

ANEMONE

Four to five straight stitches form a petal

RIBBON FLOWER

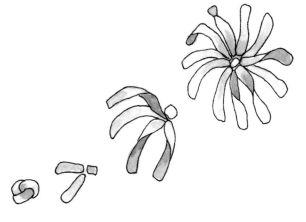

The lazy daisy leaves, straight stitch leaves and french knots are worked in dark green 3 mm ribbon. If this is hard to come by, choose a dark green wool such as Appletons crewel no. 348. The ribbon, however, adds life and sheen to the design and is worth tracking down.

Beading

A double strand of machine cotton is a good idea for beading to give strength. You will need a beading needle, or a no. 9 or 10 straw needle, to fit through the holes in the beads. Secure the cotton with a couple of back stitches into the centre of a hibiscus. Put the needle through the hole in the middle of a sequin, then through a small pearl. Now take the needle back down through the hole in the sequin and into the centre of the flower, pulling the thread tight so that the pearl lies on top of the sequin and the sequin lies in the centre of the flower. Fasten off the thread on the wrong side with several back stitches.

The anenomes have a pearl in the centre of each, daisies have a diamanté, asters a pale blue pearl, and ribbon flowers a silver glass bead. Your choice will depend, of course, on the availability of various beads and these are only suggested as a guide.

I also dotted a few sequins, glass beads and pearls at random to add a bit of interest. When you have finished, remove the tacking thread.

I hope you have as much fun making this beaded sweater as I did.

RIBBON LEAVES

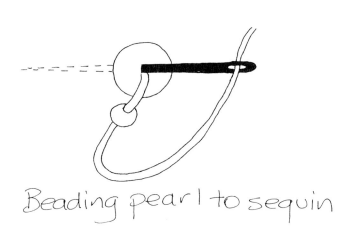

Beading pearl to sequin

140

Index of stitches and techniques

As all stitches and techniques have been illustrated alongside the explanation, diagrams have not been separately indexed.

Glossary of terms

Making up...*finishing*
Tacking...*basting*
Knickers...*underpants or panties*
Press studs...*snaps*
Straw needles...*milliner's needles*
Haberdashery...*fabric store*
Face washer...*face cloth*
Anti-clockwise...*counter-clockwise*
Wadding...*batting*
Reef knot...*square knot*
Sloppy Joe...*sweat shirt*